The Ultimate
English Monarchs Quiz

B.R. Egginton

<u>**Contents**</u>

Preface

'The saddest thing about any man is that he be ignorant, and the most exciting thing is that he knows.'
Alfred the Great

'The upward course of a nation's history is due, in the long run, to the soundless heart of its average men and women.'
Elizabeth II

From the fearful to the just, the warlike to the learned and the sane to the downright mad, the monarchs who have ruled England for centuries are far from being an endless succession of forgettable grey-haired men.

Boy kings have sat upon the throne (locked up by those closest to them, never to be seen again), as have a succession of female titans (fending off armadas and burning all those who dared defy the 'one true faith') and let's not forget the warriors (fighting to the death and even then demanding that their bodies be embalmed to lead their troops into battle).

Over time the role of the monarchy has evolved dramatically: transitioning from an absolute ruler to a constitutional figurehead.

After the signing of the Magna Carta in 1215, the first seeds of democracy were sown; long before the celebrated French Revolution and the Thirteen Colonies' equivalent across the Atlantic.

Other episodes in the long march of progress were more bloody: the overthrow of Richard II's 'tyranny', Jack Cade's Rebellion and the beheading of Charles I just to name a few.

In short, this is not only the story of the highs and lows of a succession of privileged individuals, but of the entire English nation: the home of the world's most formidable navy, the mother of the largest empire in human history and the founder of the contemporary age's predominant language.

To learn more about the grand and dastardly deeds of England's purest bloodline, look inside!

Questions

Alfred the Great (easy)

Q1 Alfred the Great became King of what in 871?

A Mercia
B Wessex
C East Anglia
D Kent

Q2 What army did Alfred the Great defeat at the Battle of Edington?

A Norman Army
B Spanish Armada
C Great Heathen Army
D Scottish Army

Q3 The Treaty of Wedmore was an agreement between Alfred the Great and what other leader?

A Macbeth, King of Scotland
B Guthrum
C Harald Hardrada
D Cnut the Great

Q4 Alfred the Great was the first ruler to style himself King of what?

A The Christians
B The Angles
C The Britons
D The Anglo-Saxons

Q5 What Welsh monk wrote the *Life of King Alfred* in the 9th century?

A Nennius
B Asser
C Gildas
D Bede

Q6 In what English city does a famous statue of Alfred the Great stand?

A York
B Northampton
C Wolverhampton
D Winchester

Q7 How many other English kings are referred to as 'The Great'?

A 0
B 1
C 3
D 8

Q8 Where was Alfred the Great buried?

A Westminster Abbey
B York Minster
C Leicester Cathedral
D Hyde Abbey

Q9 According to the *Anglo-Saxon Chronicle* what city was Alfred the Great sent to in 853?

A Dublin
B London
C Paris
D Rome

Q10 What relation succeeded Alfred the Great as king?

A Son
B Nephew
C Brother
D Uncle

Alfred the Great (average)

Q1 Who was Alfred the Great's father?

Q2 What Anglo-Saxon kingdom was the dominant power in Britain prior to the rise of the Kingdom of Wessex?

Q3 How many of Alfred the Great's brothers served as King of Wessex?

Q4 Alfred the Great had the Viking leader Guthrum converted to what religion?

Q5 What was the name of Alfred the Great's mother?

Q6 What was the name of Alfred the Great's wife?

Q7 Alfred the Great had to deal with what crisis at the start of his reign?

Q8 The *Doom Book* was a code of what?

Q9 Alfred the Great proposed primary education be conducted in what language?

Q10 Alfred the Great is celebrated as a passionate supporter of what?

Alfred the Great (expert)

Q1 In what year did the Battle of Ashdown take place?

Q2 What is the Burghal Hidage?

Q3 What was a *herepath*?

Q4 Alfred the Great translated what treatise by Pope Gregory I?

Q5 In what century is *The Proverbs of Alfred* believed to have been written?

Q6 The Alfred Jewel was discovered in what English county?

Q7 In what year did Alfred the Great die?

Q8 Who was Alfred the Great's eldest daughter?

Q9 What renaissance took place during the 8th and 9th centuries?

Q10 Launched in 1901, what type of ship was the HMS *King Alfred*?

Edward the Elder (easy)

Q1 How was Alfred the Great related to Edward the Elder?

A Uncle
B Cousin
C Father
D Grandfather

Q2 How many times did Edward the Elder marry?

A 0
B 1
C 2
D 3

Q3 What royal house was Edward the Elder a member of?

A House of York
B House of Blois
C House of Wessex
D House of Tudor

Q4 What was Edward the Elder's title?

A King of the English
B King of the Anglo-Saxons
C King of Wessex
D King of England

Q5 Where did Edward the Elder's coronation take place?

A Canterbury
B Winchester
C Kingston upon Thames
D Hastings

Q6 In what year did Æthelwold's Revolt break out?

A 889
B 899
C 904
D 912

Q7 Edward the Elder's forces defeated an army of Northumbrian Vikings at what battle in 910?

A Battle of Tettenhall
B Battle of Culloden
C Battle of Bannockburn
D Battle of Tewkesbury

Q8 How many of Edward the Elder's children served as king?

A 0
B 1
C 2
D 3

Q9 What English county did Edward the Elder die in?

A Staffordshire
B Wiltshire
C Cheshire
D Berkshire

Q10 Edward the Elder was called 'the Elder' to distinguish him from what other king?

A Edward Longshanks
B Edward II
C Edward the Martyr
D Edward the Confessor

Edward the Elder (average)

Q1 Who challenged Edward the Elder's claim to the throne when he became king?

Q2 Ætheling was a term used to describe princes who were eligible for what?

Q3 Edward the Elder had the bones of what saint seized in 909?

Q4 What position did Plegmund hold during Edward the Elder's reign?

Q5 What Benedictine abbey was founded in Winchester in 901?

Q6 What relation was Eadgifu of Kent to Edward the Elder?

Q7 What title did Edward the Elder's sister, Æthelflæd, hold?

Q8 While Alfred the Great excelled at learning, what did Edward the Elder excel at?

Q9 In what year did the Battle of Buttington take place?

Q10 The original manuscript of *The Anglo-Saxon Chronicle* was created in what century?

Edward the Elder (expert)

Q1 In what years did Edward the Elder's reign take place?

Q2 In what year did the Battle of the Holme take place?

Q3 Who did Edward the Elder marry around the year 893?

Q4 In what decade was Edward the Elder born?

Q5 What was Badbury Rings?

Q6 What kingdom was dissolved in 918?

Q7 The body of which daughter of Edward the Elder was discovered by archaeologists in 2008?

Q8 What was the name of the Lord of the Mercians who died in 911?

Q9 What post did Frithestan hold?

Q10 What former advisor to Alfred the Great died in 901?

Æthelstan (average)

Q1 Æthelstan was the first Anglo-Saxon king to rule over the whole of what?

Q2 What country did Æthelstan invade in 934?

Q3 What battle did Æthelstan fight against Olaf Guthfrithson in 937?

Q4 What did Æthelstan conquer in 927?

Q5 Where was Æthelstan buried?

Q6 How was Æthelstan related to his successor, Edmund I?

Q7 *Armes Prydein* is a prophetic poem originating from what country?

Q8 What name is given by historians to the unknown scribe who drafted charters by which Æthelstan made grants of land between 928 and 935?

Q9 What was the occupation of Israel the Grammarian?

Q10 What language is the poem *Battle of Brunanburh* written in?

Edmund I (average)

Q1 How was Edmund I related to Alfred the Great?

Q2 Edmund I was assassinated while attending what?

Q3 How many times did Edmund I marry?

Q4 How was Edmund I related to Olaf of York?

Q5 What territory did Edmund I cede to Malcolm I of Scotland?

Q6 Edmund I played a key role in the restoration of what French king?

Q7 In what village was Edmund I assassinated?

Q8 Who was Edmund I's sister, Eadgyth, married to?

Q9 How was Edmund I's successor, Eadred, related to him?

Q10 Where is the Coronation Stone located?

Eadred (average)

Q1 How was Eadred's successor, Eadwig, related to him?

Q2 How many times did Eadred marry?

Q3 Who was Archbishop of Canterbury during Eadred's reign?

Q4 Eadred brought the whole of what kingdom under his control?

Q5 Eadred is believed to have died from what kind of illness?

Q6 As well as being King of Norway, Eric Bloodaxe also served as King of what?

Q7 Where are Eadred's bones now buried?

Q8 In what years did Eadred serve as King of the English?

Q9 Where did Eadred's coronation take place?

Q10 Who was Eadred's mother?

Eadwig (average)

Q1 What was Eadwig's nickname?

Q2 How old was Eadwig when he became king?

Q3 Who was Eadwig's mother?

Q4 Who wrote the play *Edwy and Elgiva*?

Q5 What future Archbishop of Canterbury was forced into exile shortly after Eadwig's coronation?

Q6 Eadwig's marriage to who was annulled?

Q7 What city did Eadwig die in?

Q8 After leading nobles divided the kingdom in 957, Eadwig remained king south of what river?

Q9 Why did Eadwig leave his coronation banquet?

Q10 In what year did Eadwig's reign end?

Edgar (average)

Q1 What was Edgar's nickname?

Q2 Who was Edgar's father?

Q3 What position was Dunstan notably appointed to during Edgar's reign?

Q4 Where was Edgar crowned king?

Q5 Who did Edgar allegedly murder in order to marry their wife?

Q6 In what village can the Dead Man's Plack be found?

Q7 A council was held in what city shortly after Edgar's coronation?

Q8 Where was Edgar buried?

Q9 What royal house was Edgar a member of?

Q10 The main elements of the coronation oath of the British monarch can be traced to Edgar's coronation. Who devised it?

Edward the Martyr (average)

Q1 When Edward the Martyr became king, who was a rival claimant to the throne?

Q2 At what castle did Edward the Martyr die?

Q3 Why did some people oppose Edward the Martyr becoming king?

Q4 What two senior figures in the Church supported Edward the Martyr's claim to the throne?

Q5 What caused Edward the Martyr's death in 978?

Q6 In what three Churches is Edward the Martyr recognised as a saint?

Q7 On what day of the year is Edward the Martyr's feast day?

Q8 Where are the relics of Edward the Martyr kept?

Q9 In what years did Edward the Martyr rule England?

Q10 Ælfhere held what title during Edward the Martyr's reign?

Æthelred the Unready (average)

Q1 How many times did Æthelred the Unready serve as King of the English?

Q2 What does the name Æthelred mean?

Q3 In what year did the Battle of Maldon take place?

Q4 What name was given to the tax that was raised to pay tribute to Viking raiders?

Q5 The St. Brice's Day massacre involved the killing of what group of people?

Q6 Who invaded England in 1013?

Q7 Æthelred the Unready's reign of approximately 37 years was the longest in English history until it was surpassed by which king?

Q8 Who was the second wife of Æthelred the Unready?

Q9 Gunhilde was the sister of what future King of the English?

Q10 In what city did Æthelred the Unready die?

Sweyn Forkbeard (average)

Q1 In what years did Sweyn Forkbeard serve as King of England?

Q2 Who was Sweyn Forkbeard's father?

Q3 Sweyn Forkbeard served as King of what from 986 until his death?

Q4 Who succeeded Sweyn Forkbeard as King of England?

Q5 In what sea was the Battle of Svolder fought?

Q6 Sweyn Forkbeard's invasion of England is believed to have been partly motivated by revenge for what 1002 massacre?

Q7 Which son of Sweyn Forkbeard would later become King of England?

Q8 Sweyn Forkbeard was a member of what royal house?

Q9 Before she married Sweyn Forkbeard, who was Sigrid the Haughty's husband?

Q10 Where did Æthelred the Unready flee into exile when Sweyn Forkbeard seized control of England?

Edmund Ironside (average)

Q1 In what year did Edmund Ironside serve as King of England?

Q2 Who was Ealdorman of Mercia during Edmund Ironside's reign?

Q3 What was the name of Edmund Ironside's wife?

Q4 Who was Edmund Ironside's wife previously married to?

Q5 In what battle did Cnut the Great defeat Edmund Ironside?

Q6 What were Edmund Ironside's two sons called?

Q7 Where was Edmund Ironside buried?

Q8 Some historians believe the Elizabethan play *Edmund Ironside* is an early work of which famous playwright?

Q9 Edmund Ironside's granddaughter, Margaret, married what king?

Q10 How old was Edmund Ironside when he died?

Cnut the Great (easy)

Q1 What name was given to the territories governed by Cnut the Great?

A Scandinavia
B Jorvik
C North Sea Empire
D Vikingland

Q2 Who was Cnut the Great's father?

A Edmund Ironside
B Harald Bluetooth
C Æthelred the Unready
D Sweyn Forkbeard

Q3 How many of Cnut the Great's children went on to become King of England?

A 0
B 1
C 2
D 3

Q4 As well as being King of England, what other kingdoms did Cnut the Great rule over?

A Denmark and Norway
B Denmark and Iceland
C Norway and Sweden
D Holy Roman Empire and Castile

Q5 Who was Cnut the Great's second wife, Emma of Normandy, previously married to?

A Edmund Ironside
B Harald II of Denmark
C Æthelred the Unready
D Edward the Martyr

Q6 In what year did the Battle of Assandun take place?

A 1002
B 1016
C 1022
D 1041

Q7 Who was Archbishop of Canterbury when Cnut the Great became King of England?

A Thomas Becket
B Lyfing
C Æthelnoth
D Robert of Jumièges

Q8 In what year did the Battle of Helgeå take place?

A 999
B 1010
C 1026
D 1040

Q9 Whose coronation did Cnut the Great attend in 1027?

A Harald II of Denmark
B Rudolph III of Burgundy
C Olof Skötkonung, King of Sweden
D Conrad II, Holy Roman Emperor

Q10 What was Sigvatr Þórðarson's occupation?

A General
B Poet
C Merchant
D Diplomat

Cnut the Great (average)

Q1 The story *King Canute and the tide* was recorded by what 12th century historian?

Q2 Who did Cnut the Great succeed as King of Denmark?

Q3 Who was Cnut the Great's first wife?

Q4 Who did Cnut the Great defeat at the Battle of Assandun?

Q5 Which Ealdorman of Mercia was killed on Cnut the Great's orders in 1017?

Q6 What position did Cnut the Great appoint his brother in law, Ulf, to?

Q7 What was the capital city of Norway at the time of Cnut the Great?

Q8 In what country did the Battle of Stiklestad take place?

Q9 What city did Cnut the Great travel to in 1027?

Q10 Who succeeded Cnut the Great as King of Norway?

Cnut the Great (expert)

Q1 In what years did Cnut the Great serve as King of England?

Q2 In what English county did the Battle of Assandun take place?

Q3 Shortly before Edmund Ironside's death it was agreed Cnut the Great would rule all territory north of what river?

Q4 In what year did Cnut the Great become King of Denmark?

Q5 Who was King of Norway between 1015 and 1028?

Q6 Where did Cnut the Great die?

Q7 What royal house was Cnut the Great a member of?

Q8 How many administrative units did Cnut the Great divide England into?

Q9 Godwin was made Earl of what by Cnut the Great?

Q10 Where are Cnut the Great's bones now buried?

Harold I (average)

Q1 What was Harold I's nickname?

Q2 Who was supposed to become King of England upon Cnut the Great's death?

Q3 Which Archbishop of Canterbury was reluctant to proclaim Harold I king?

Q4 What title did Harold I's supporter Leofric hold?

Q5 What was the name of the Earl of Wessex who opposed Harold I's rule?

Q6 In what year did Harold I die?

Q7 What future King of England returned from exile in 1036?

Q8 Which of Æthelred the Unready's sons did Harold I have blinded, leading to his death shortly thereafter?

Q9 Where was Harold I's body originally buried?

Q10 Who is believed to have been a son of Harold I?

Harthacnut (average)

Q1 How was Harthacnut related to his predecessor, Harold I?

Q2 Before becoming King of England, what other kingdom did Harthacnut rule over?

Q3 In what years did Harthacnut serve as King of England?

Q4 Who was Harthacnut's mother?

Q5 After becoming King of England, whose body did Harthacnut have disinterred and publicly beheaded?

Q6 Lady Godiva is said to have ridden naked through the streets of what city?

Q7 How was Harthacnut related to his successor, Edward the Confessor?

Q8 Harthacnut was the last ruler from what region to rule England?

Q9 Harthacnut died while attending what?

Q10 How many times did Harthacnut marry?

Edward the Confessor (easy)

Q1 In what year did Edward the Confessor die?

A 1050
B 1062
C 1066
D 1070

Q2 Edward the Confessor was the last English king from what royal house?

A House of Knýtlinga
B House of Blois
C House of Plantagenet
D House of Wessex

Q3 Where is Edward the Confessor buried?

A Westminster Abbey
B Windsor Castle
C St Paul's Cathedral
D Tower of London

Q4 Who was Edward the Confessor's father?

A Edmund Ironside
B Cnut the Great
C Æthelred the Unready
D Unknown

Q5 Which Pope made Edward the Confessor a Saint?

A Gregory II
B Urban IV
C Pius I
D Alexander III

Q6 Where did Edward the Confessor spend some of his childhood in exile?

A Rome
B Normandy
C Scotland
D Denmark

Q7 Where did Edward the Confessor's coronation take place?

A Northampton
B Oxford
C Winchester
D Westminster

Q8 Godwin was Earl of what?

A Essex
B Wessex
C Suffolk
D Norfolk

Q9 What positon did Stigand hold between 1052 and 1070?

A Archbishop of Canterbury
B Regent
C Co-King
D Bishop of London

Q10 St Edward's Chair is known by what other name?

A Coronation Chair
B Saintly Chair
C Royal Chair
D Wessex Chair

Edward the Confessor (average)

Q1 Who was Edward the Confessor's wife?

Q2 In what village was Edward the Confessor born?

Q3 Who was Edward the Confessor's only full brother?

Q4 Who was the first Norman to serve as Archbishop of Canterbury?

Q5 What title did Tostig Godwinson hold?

Q6 Who seized control of the Scottish throne in 1040?

Q7 Who became Earl of Northumbria in 1065?

Q8 Who was Edward the Confessor's mother?

Q9 How many legitimate children did Edward the Confessor have?

Q10 Edward the Confessor appears at the start of what famous tapestry?

Edward the Confessor (expert)

Q1 What historical manuscript, completed in 1067, did Edward the Confessor's wife commission?

Q2 On what date does St Edward's feast day take place?

Q3 In what years did Edward the Confessor serve as King of England?

Q4 Edward the Confessor ordered the assassination of what Welsh prince?

Q5 Which Norwegian king invaded England shortly after Edward the Confessor's death?

Q6 As well as Edward the Confessor, what two other kings appear on the Wilton Diptych?

Q7 The *Játvarðar Saga* was compiled in what country?

Q8 In what year was Edward the Confessor's half-brother, Eadwig Ætheling, killed?

Q9 What nobleman dominated English politics at the time of Edward the Confessor's death?

Q10 What king planned on invading England in the early stages of Edward the Confessor's reign?

Harold Godwinson (average)

Q1 Harold Godwinson was killed during what battle?

Q2 In what year did Harold Godwinson serve as King of England?

Q3 In what battle was Harald Hardrada killed?

Q4 What conquest took place during Harold Godwinson's reign?

Q5 Who served as Queen consort of England during Harold Godwinson's reign?

Q6 Where is Harold Godwinson said to have been hit with an arrow?

Q7 Harold Godwinson's father was Earl of what?

Q8 What is the name of the first history of Harold Godwinson's fall from power?

Q9 Which two brothers of Harold Godwinson died alongside him in battle?

Q10 The Battle of Fulford took place near what city?

Edgar Ætheling (average)

Q1 Who elected Edgar Ætheling King of England?

Q2 What kingdom was Edgar Ætheling born in?

Q3 Who was Edgar Ætheling's father?

Q4 How many sisters did Edgar Ætheling have?

Q5 In what year did Edgar Ætheling serve as King of England?

Q6 Where was Edgar Ætheling crowned King of England?

Q7 What king was Edgar Ætheling's brother in law?

Q8 After William the Conquerors death, whose bid to become King of England did Edgar Ætheling support?

Q9 How was Edgar Ætheling related to Edgar, King of Scotland?

Q10 Edgar Ætheling was captured during what battle in 1106?

William I (easy)

Q1 Besides from 'the Conqueror', what other nickname did William I have?

A The Brave
B The Bastard
C The Cruel
D The Cunning

Q2 How many of William I's sons went on to become King of England?

A 0
B 1
C 2
D 3

Q3 In what battle did William I beat the King of England, Harold Godwinson?

A Battle of Hastings
B Battle of Stamford Bridge
C Battle of Edington
D Battle of Badon

Q4 In what town did William I die?

A Bayeux
B London
C Rouen
D York

Q5 After the Norman Conquest, what did William I change the language of government in England to?

A English
B French
C Breton
D Basque

Q6 After being crowned King of England, how long was it before William I returned to Normandy?

A 3 months
B 1 year
C 5 years
D Never

Q7 How did William I primarily consolidate his conquest?

A Military occupation
B Built castles
C Killed rival claimants
D Starved the population

Q8 Which of the following was William I not responsible for?

A Tower of London
B Reconstruction of Durham Cathedral
C Domesday Book
D Church of England

Q9 Where was William I crowned King of England?

A York Minster
B St Paul's Cathedral
C Westminster Abbey
D Reims Cathedral

Q10 Who did William I fight against at the siege and battle of Gerberoy in the winter of 1078-79?

A Robert Curthose
B William Rufus
C Harold Godwinson
D Odo of Bayeux

William I (average)

Q1 On what day of the year was William I crowned King of England?

Q2 Who was William I's wife?

Q3 Who became Duke of Normandy after William I's death?

Q4 Who did William I and the French king, Henry I, defeat at the Battle of Varaville?

Q5 In what year was the Domesday Book completed?

Q6 Which abbey did William I have constructed as penance for the bloodshed at the Battle of Hastings?

Q7 How many volumes is the Domesday Book composed of?

Q8 Who did William I appoint as Archbishop of Canterbury in 1070?

Q9 Which area of Hampshire was proclaimed a royal forest by William I?

Q10 The injury that led to William I's death is said to have occurred while he was doing what?

William I (expert)

Q1 What relation was Edward the Confessor to William I?

Q2 Who was William I's mother, Herleva, married to?

Q3 Where did William I land in England, beginning the Norman Conquest?

Q4 The Harrying of the North occurred during the winter of which years?

Q5 Where was Hereward the Wake's base when leading his rebellion against Norman rulers?

Q6 In what treaty did Malcolm III of Scotland recognise William I as his feudal overlord?

Q7 In what year did William the Conqueror become Duke of Normandy?

Q8 How many days separated the Battle of Stamford Bridge and the Battle of Hastings?

Q9 William I's half-brother Odo held what two titles?

Q10 Approximately how long is the Bayeux Tapestry (in metres)?

William II (average)

Q1 In what forest did William II die in 1100?

Q2 Why was William II also called William Rufus?

Q3 How many children did William II have?

Q4 The 'Rufus Stone' is claimed to mark what?

Q5 Who led the Rebellion of 1088?

Q6 Who did William II appoint Archbishop of Canterbury in 1093?

Q7 In 1091 William II repulsed an invasion by which Scottish king?

Q8 William II's older brother, Robert Curthose, took part in which crusade?

Q9 The earliest reference to William II's death is in which chronicle?

Q10 Which cathedral was William II buried in?

Henry I (easy)

Q1 What was the name of the ship that sank in 1120, killing Henry I's son and heir William Adelin?

A The *White Ship*
B The *Black Ship*
C *Queen Anne's Revenge*
D HMS *Victory*

Q2 How many times did Henry I marry?

A 0
B 1
C 2
D 3

Q3 What was the name of the period of civil war that followed Henry I's death?

A Wars of the Roses
B English Civil War
C Glorious Revolution
D The Anarchy

Q4 How many brothers did Henry I have?

A 0
B 1
C 3
D 4

Q5 After his father's death, where did Henry I initially live?

A England
B France
C Scotland
D Normandy

Q6 During his coronation, Henry I promised a return to the gentler customs of which former English king?

A William I
B Alfred the Great
C Edward the Confessor
D Edward the Martyr

Q7 *The Charter of Liberties* is known by what other name?

A *The Coronation Charter*
B *The Great Charter*
C *The Royal Charter*
D *The People's Charter*

Q8 Which royal house did Henry I belong to?

A Tudor
B Stuart
C Normandy
D Plantagenet

Q9 In what year did Henry I die?

A 1066
B 1100
C 1120
D 1135

Q10 What happened to Ranulf Flambard, Bishop of Durham on Henry I's rise to power?

A Imprisoned
B Executed
C Baptised
D Betrothed

Henry I (average)

Q1 In what duchy did Henry I die?

Q2 Which relative did Henry defeat at the Battle of Tinchebray?

Q3 What was the primary motivation behind Henry I's decision to marry Adeliza of Louvain in 1121?

Q4 How many years after the Norman Conquest was Henry I born?

Q5 Why wasn't Robert Curthose present to claim the throne of England when William II died?

Q6 What was the name of Henry I's first legitimate child?

Q7 Henry I had a dispute with which Archbishop of Canterbury in the early stages of his reign?

Q8 Who did Henry I betroth his eldest daughter to in 1108?

Q9 The Battle of Brémule was fought between Henry I and who?

Q10 According to the chronicler Henry of Huntingdon, eating too much what caused Henry I's death?

Henry I (expert)

Q1 Where was Henry I buried?

Q2 Who crowned Henry I king?

Q3 In what year was the Treaty of Alton signed?

Q4 In what year did Henry I replace his elder brother, Robert Curthose, as Duke of Normandy?

Q5 What did Henry I keep at Woodstock Palace?

Q6 The oldest surviving Pipe Roll dates from what year of Henry I's reign?

Q7 Who was the captain of the ship that sank in 1120, killing William Adelin?

Q8 William Adelin was married to the eldest daughter of which count?

Q9 William Rufus's chancellor, William Giffard, became Bishop of what on Henry I's rise to power?

Q10 What are the names of the two kings who ruled France during Henry I's reign?

Stephen and Matilda (easy)

Q1 What was the name of the civil war that took place during Stephen's reign?

A Wars of the Roses
B The Anarchy
C English Civil War
D Glorious Revolution

Q2 What relation was Henry I to Stephen?

A Father
B Brother
C Cousin
D Uncle

Q3 Matilda's second husband was the founder of which royal house?

A Plantagenet
B Tudor
C Blois
D Normandy

Q4 Who was captured at the Battle of Lincoln (1141)?

A King Stephen
B Empress Matilda
C Henry II
D Robert FitzRoy, Earl of Gloucester

Q5 How many children did Matilda have with her first husband?

A 0
B 1
C 2
D 5

Q6 Which crusade was fought during Stephen's reign?

A First Crusade
B Second Crusade
C Third Crusade
D Fourth Crusade

Q7 Matilda's mother, Matilda of Scotland, was originally christened with what name?

A Elizabeth
B Mary
C Edith
D Alexandra

Q8 Where is Matilda buried?

A Tower of London
B Windsor Castle
C Westminster Abbey
D Rouen Cathedral

Q9 In what year did Matilda cease to be Empress of the Holy Roman Empire?

A 1125
B 1135
C 1154
D 1167

Q10 Stephen and the future Henry II sealed the treaty that ended 18 years of civil war with a kiss of what?

A Affection
B Allegiance
C Peace
D Unity

Stephen and Matilda (average)

Q1 King Stephen is often referred to by what other name?

Q2 What was the name of Stephen's eldest son?

Q3 The Treaty of Wallingford ensured who would succeed Stephen as King of England?

Q4 Whose death caused a succession crisis?

Q5 The renowned historical source *Gesta Stephani* means roughly what in English?

Q6 Matilda died during which king's reign?

Q7 William of Ypres was a key military leader, loyal to who?

Q8 Stephen's wife was a member of which royal house?

Q9 Because she was never crowned Queen of England, what title has Matilda been given instead?

Q10 Matilda's half-brother Robert was Earl of what?

Stephen and Matilda (expert)

Q1 Between what years did the Anarchy occur?

Q2 Who led King Stephen's army at the Rout of Winchester?

Q3 Matilda fled from which castle, closely avoiding capture, in the winter of 1141-42?

Q4 In which abbey was Stephen buried?

Q5 Stephen's father was Count of what?

Q6 Where was Matilda crowned Holy Roman Empress?

Q7 Which Archbishop of Canterbury crowned Stephen King of England?

Q8 How many of Stephen's legitimate children lived into adulthood?

Q9 At which battle was Stephen's father killed?

Q10 Who was heir apparent to the English throne before Stephen agreed to adopt the future Henry II as his heir?

Henry II (easy)

Q1 How many of Henry II's sons went on to become King of England?

A 1
B 2
C 3
D 4

Q2 Henry II famously clashed with which Archbishop of Canterbury?

A Thomas Becket
B Hubert Walter
C Simon Sudbury
D Edmund of Abingdon

Q3 Henry II was the first person from which royal house to serve as King of England?

A Normandy
B Blois
C Plantagenet
D Orange-Nassau

Q4 Henry II was born in and died in which kingdom?

A Kingdom of England
B Kingdom of France
C Kingdom of Castile
D Kingdom of Bohemia

Q5 What colour hair is Henry II said to have had?

A Brown
B Black
C Blond
D Red

Q6 Which two languages did Henry II primarily speak?

A English and French
B English and Latin
C French and Latin
D French and Greek

Q7 In which cathedral did King Stephen announce the Treaty of Winchester?

A St Paul's Cathedral
B York Minster
C Winchester Cathedral
D Salisbury Cathedral

Q8 Where did Henry II invade in 1171?

A Scotland
B Ireland
C Wales
D France

Q9 What happened to Eleanor of Aquitaine between 1173 and 1189?

A Returned to Aquitaine
B Excommunicated
C On pilgrimage
D Imprisoned

Q10 Which holy city fell to Islamic forces in 1187?

A Jerusalem
B Rome
C Nazareth
D Bethlehem

Henry II (average)

Q1 What was the name of Henry II's wife?

Q2 Which son did Henry II discover had betrayed him just before he died?

Q3 Which treaty paved the way for Henry II being named King of England?

Q4 What was Henry II's nickname?

Q5 Who was King of France for the majority of Henry II's reign?

Q6 Henry II was the first ruler of which empire?

Q7 What did Henry II die from?

Q8 Ruaidrí Ua Conchobair was named what in 1166?

Q9 Which pope canonised Thomas Becket?

Q10 Henry II's father was Count of what?

Henry II (expert)

Q1 Where did Henry II die?

Q2 In what years did Henry the Young King serve as Junior King of England?

Q3 How many knights are said to have been involved in the murder of Thomas Becket?

Q4 Why was Adrian IV becoming pope in 1154 significant?

Q5 The Constitutions of Clarendon were passed by Henry II in what year?

Q6 Which Cambridge clerk almost had his arm chopped off when he tried to defend Thomas Becket?

Q7 Which king was captured at the Battle of Alnwick?

Q8 Which four close relatives of Henry II were involved in the Revolt of 1173–74?

Q9 *Tractatus de legibus et consuetudinibus regni Anglie* is the earliest treatise on what?

Q10 In which abbey is Henry II buried?

Richard I (easy)

Q1 Approximately how long did Richard I spend in England during his 10-year reign?

A 6 months
B 1 year
C 3 years
D 9 years

Q2 What was Richard I's nickname?

A The Bold
B The Patriot
C The Lionheart
D The Spendthrift

Q3 Which crusade was Richard I involved in?

A First
B Second
C Third
D Fourth

Q4 Richard I is often depicted as being the favourite of which relative?

A His mother
B His father
C His eldest brother
D His youngest sister

Q5 The Massacre of Ayyadieh occurred after the fall of which city?

A Acre
B Jerusalem
C Damascus
D Constantinople

Q6 In what year did Richard I become Duke of Normandy?

A 1175
B 1180
C 1189
D Never

Q7 In which kingdom did the Archbishop Canterbury, Baldwin of Forde, die?

A Kingdom of England
B Kingdom of France
C Kingdom of Castile
D Kingdom of Jerusalem

Q8 In 1190 a major massacre of Jews occurred in which city?

A Winchester
B Salisbury
C Norwich
D York

Q9 Richard I fought in the Battle of Arsuf against who?

A Philip II of France
B John of England
C Baldwin V of Jerusalem
D Saladin

Q10 The Knights Templar's allegiance was to which ruler?

A King of England
B King of France
C King of Jerusalem
D The Pope

Richard I (average)

Q1 In what duchy did Richard I die?

Q2 Who was Richard I's wife?

Q3 Which French king did Richard I go on crusade with?

Q4 Who was Richard I's main opponent whilst on crusade?

Q5 On Richard I's accession to the throne of England what position did William de Longchamp acquire?

Q6 Richard I and his brothers frequently rebelled against who?

Q7 Which group were the victims of serious prejudice during Richard I's reign?

Q8 What island did Richard I of England and Philip II of France arrive at in September 1190?

Q9 In which city was Richard I's heart buried?

Q10 Richard I was killed with what weapon?

Richard I (expert)

Q1 In which abbey is Richard I buried?

Q2 After being captured by Leopold V, Duke of Austria, what castle was Richard I held in?

Q3 Who was Richard I's wet nurse?

Q4 The *Itinerarium Regis Ricardi* is a Latin prose narrative of what?

Q5 The scholar Jacob of Orléans was killed in London during what?

Q6 The Saladin tithe was raised in response to what?

Q7 What was the proper title of the Sheriff of Nottingham during Richard I's reign?

Q8 Who was designated heir to the throne of England in 1190?

Q9 Isaac Komnenos ruled which island before Richard I invaded it in 1191?

Q10 Richard I was married in which city?

John (easy)

Q1 What does Magna Carta mean in English?

A Great Charter
B Great Change
C Great Constitution
D Great Crimes

Q2 What was King John's nickname?

A The Fearless
B The Foolish
C Lackland
D The Cruel

Q3 King John was the youngest son of which King of England?

A William II
B Henry I
C Henry II
D Richard I

Q4 Which pope excommunicated King John in 1209?

A Innocent III
B Urban II
C Gregory I
D Benedict V

Q5 How many times did King John marry?

A 0
B 1
C 2
D 3

Q6 What did King John die from?

A Wounds in battle
B Dysentery
C Heart attack
D Liver failure

Q7 Who was King of Scotland for the majority of King John's reign?

A Alexander II
B Alexander III
C James IV
D William the Lion

Q8 Where was the Magna Carta agreed?

A Smithfield
B Runneymede
C Tower of London
D Nottingham Castle

Q9 Who became Archbishop of Canterbury in 1207?

A Thomas Becket
B Walter d'Eynsham
C Ralph Neville
D Stephen Langton

Q10 Which war resulted from King John's refusal to abide by the Magna Carta?

A The First Barons' War
B The Second Barons' War
C The Hundred Years' War
D The Anglo-French War

John (average)

Q1 King John was buried in which city?

Q2 King John is regarded as being the last ruler of which empire?

Q3 King John became Lord of what in 1177?

Q4 The Treaty of Le Goulet was signed between King John and which other ruler?

Q5 King John is associated with which legendary outlaw?

Q6 King John is commonly regarded as the favourite of which relative?

Q7 Which claimant to the English throne is believed to have been killed on King John's orders?

Q8 King John wanted John de Gray to be appointed to what position in the Church?

Q9 Which future French king was involved in the First Barons' War?

Q10 What did King John lose just before his death?

John (expert)

Q1 The Battle of Bouvines was the concluding battle of what war?

Q2 King John had his marriage to who annulled in 1199?

Q3 When Richard I became King of England, John was granted extensive lands in an attempt to do what?

Q4 How did Arthur I, Duke of Brittany have a claim to the English throne?

Q5 How many legitimate children did King John have?

Q6 In what years did the French invasion of Normandy take place?

Q7 William de Braose was what kind of lord?

Q8 William Marshal, Earl of Pembroke was a knight who served which five English kings?

Q9 King John married his illegitimate daughter Joan to which Welsh prince?

Q10 Which uprising occurred in 1211?

Henry III (average)

Q1 Henry III was known by what other name?

Q2 Henry III inherited the English throne in the middle of what war?

Q3 What kingdom did Henry III invade in 1230?

Q4 Who was Henry III's wife?

Q5 Simon de Montfort was Earl of what?

Q6 Henry III adopted which former English king as his patron saint?

Q7 The Statute of Jewry attempted to segregate which group?

Q8 In what year were the Provisions of Westminster drawn up?

Q9 Which key nobleman was killed at the Battle of Evesham?

Q10 Which short-lived university was founded by Henry III in 1261?

Edward I (average)

Q1 Edward I had the Eleanor crosses erected in memory of who?

Q2 What were Edward I's two nicknames?

Q3 The Edict of Expulsion was a royal decree issued by Edward I expelling what group from England?

Q4 Edward I launched a conquest of what country in the early stages of his reign?

Q5 The Auld Alliance was an alliance between what two kingdoms?

Q6 Which crusade did Edward I take part in?

Q7 What title did Llywelyn ap Gruffudd possess until his death in 1282?

Q8 Edward I is credited with launching an extensive building project of what in Wales?

Q9 Which war broke out in 1296?

Q10 Where was William Wallace executed?

Edward II (average)

Q1 How was Edward II allegedly murdered?

Q2 Which nobleman, originating from Gascony, did Edward II have a controversial relationship with?

Q3 Edward II's army was defeated by which Scottish king at the Battle of Bannockburn?

Q4 Edward II's wife famously had an affair with which nobleman?

Q5 Which father and son favourites of Edward II were executed in 1326?

Q6 In what year was the Battle of Boroughbridge fought?

Q7 Where is Edward II buried?

Q8 Who did Edward II abdicate in favour of?

Q9 Which regulations passed in 1311 aimed to restrict the powers of the king?

Q10 Thomas, Earl of Lancaster was executed near which castle?

Edward III (average)

Q1 Which long-lasting conflict began during Edward III's reign?

Q2 Edward III started to rule independently when he had Roger Mortimer arrested at which castle in 1330?

Q3 How was Alice Perrers associated with Edward III?

Q4 What reached England in 1348?

Q5 For much of his life Edward III was a claimant to which throne?

Q6 What was the name of Edward III's eldest son?

Q7 Who was Edward III's wife?

Q8 Which two major military victories occurred during Edward III's reign?

Q9 The Battle of Sluys was what kind of battle?

Q10 The Treaty of Brétigny was agreed between Edward III and which other king?

Richard II (easy)

Q1 What was the personal symbol of Richard II?

A Lion
B White Boar
C White Hart
D Golden Eagle

Q2 The portrait of Richard II – the oldest surviving portrait of an English monarch – is on display where?

A British Museum
B Buckingham Palace
C Windsor Castle
D Westminster Abbey

Q3 How long did Richard II survive after being deposed?

A Under a year
B 2 years
C 10 years
D 20 years

Q4 Richard II was the grandson of which English king?

A Edward I
B Edward II
C Edward III
D Richard I

Q5 How old was Richard II when the Peasants' Revolt broke out?

A 4
B 14
C 22
D 38

Q6 In which castle did Richard II die?

A Pontefract Castle
B Middleham Castle
C Tower of London
D Nottingham Castle

Q7 What was the name of the schism that occurred in the Catholic Church during Richard II's reign?

A The Roman Schism
B Pope Urban's Schism
C The Western Schism
D King Richard's Schism

Q8 What country did Richard II invade in July 1385?

A Ireland
B Scotland
C France
D Norway

Q9 How was Anne of Bohemia related to Richard II?

A Wife
B Sister
C Mother
D Aunt

Q10 The period 1397-99 is often referred to by historians as what?

A The Revolution
B The Age of Absolutism
C The Tyranny
D The Terror

Richard II (average)

Q1 How many times did Richard II marry?

Q2 Who was Richard II's father?

Q3 Which rebel leader did Richard II confront at Smithfield?

Q4 Which hall was extensively rebuilt during Richard II's reign?

Q5 *The Canterbury Tales* was written by which author during Richard II's reign?

Q6 What type of tax sparked the Peasants' Revolt?

Q7 What was the name of the Archbishop of Canterbury who was executed during the Peasants' Revolt?

Q8 What long-lasting war with France continued throughout Richard II's reign?

Q9 Thomas of Woodstock, Duke of Gloucester was murdered in which port town?

Q10 Who were the three original Lords Appellant?

Richard II (expert)

Q1 Richard II's mother, Joan, was known as the 'Fair Maid' of which English county?

Q2 What was the name of John of Gaunt's London residence, which was burnt down during the Peasants' Revolt?

Q3 What is Thomas Walsingham known for?

Q4 In what year did the Wonderful Parliament take place?

Q5 What was the name of the Lord Mayor of London who killed Wat Tyler?

Q6 In what year did the Merciless Parliament take place?

Q7 Where was Richard II born?

Q8 How old was Richard II when he came to power?

Q9 In what year did Richard II invade Ireland?

Q10 Richard II's second wife, Isabella of Valois, was the daughter of which king?

Henry IV (average)

Q1 Henry IV was known by what other name?

Q2 What relation was Richard II to Henry IV?

Q3 Which other English king was born in the same year as Henry IV (1367)?

Q4 Henry IV was the first person from which royal house to be King of England?

Q5 Which powerful nobleman was Henry IV's father?

Q6 How many times did Henry IV marry?

Q7 In what years did the Epiphany Rising occur?

Q8 Henry IV was a member of which group of noblemen during the reign of Richard II?

Q9 Henry IV defeated a rebel army led by who at the Battle of Shrewsbury?

Q10 Where was Henry IV buried?

Henry V (average)

Q1 By what other name was Henry V known?

Q2 In what year did the Battle of Agincourt take place?

Q3 What was agreed in the Treaty of Troyes?

Q4 What was John Bradmore's occupation at Henry V's court?

Q5 The estranged friend of Henry V, John Oldcastle, was associated with which religious movement?

Q6 The Treaty of Canterbury was a diplomatic agreement between the Kingdom of England and which empire?

Q7 The Siege of Harfleur occurred in what year?

Q8 What is Henry V believed to have died from?

Q9 How many children did Henry V have?

Q10 The Southampton Plot of 1415 was a conspiracy to replace Henry V with who as King of England?

Henry VI (easy)

Q1 As well as being King of England, what other kingdom did Henry VI rule?

A Kingdom of France
B Kingdom of Navarre
C Kingdom of Castile
D Kingdom of Portugal

Q2 How many children did Henry VI have?

A 0
B 1
C 3
D 8

Q3 Which church was Henry VI a member of?

A Anglican
B Catholic
C Methodist
D Orthodox

Q4 How was Joan of Arc executed?

A Stoned
B Hung, drawn and quartered
C Burned at the stake
D Guillotined

Q5 Which civil war broke out during Henry VI's reign?

A The Anarchy
B The Glorious Revolution
C The English Civil War
D The Wars of the Roses

Q6 Which royal house was Henry VI a member of?

A York
B Lancaster
C Blois
D Orange-Nassau

Q7 William Shakespeare's *Henry VI* consists of how many plays?

A 1
B 2
C 3
D 4

Q8 Henry VI suffered from bouts of what?

A Depression
B Paranoia
C Madness
D Rage

Q9 Where was William de la Pole executed?

A Tower of London
B Pontefract Castle
C Tyburn
D English Channel

Q10 The Loveday of 1458 took place at which cathedral?

A St Paul's Cathedral
B Winchester Cathedral
C Salisbury Cathedral
D Leicester Cathedral

Henry VI (average)

Q1 Who was Henry VI's wife?

Q2 Where did Henry VI die?

Q3 On how many occasions did Henry VI serve as King of England?

Q4 Where was Henry VI crowned King of France?

Q5 What was the name of Henry VI's heir?

Q6 Henry VI was liberated from his state of imprisonment in which 1461 battle?

Q7 Henry VI is buried in which castle?

Q8 Who paid the ransom for Margaret of Anjou's release in 1475?

Q9 How old was Henry VI when he became King of England?

Q10 Which long-lasting war ended during Henry VI's reign?

Henry VI (expert)

Q1 Which three educational establishments did Henry VI establish?

Q2 What was Joan of Arc's nickname?

Q3 Who was declared Regent of France following the death of Henry V?

Q4 The Congress of Arras was held in what year?

Q5 The favourite of Henry VI, William de la Pole, was Duke of what?

Q6 Jack Cade's Rebellion occurred in what year?

Q7 The Readeption refers to what event?

Q8 Who is Margaret of Anjou buried next to?

Q9 At which 1460 battle was Henry VI captured?

Q10 What relation was Charles VI (the Mad) of France to Henry VI?

Edward IV (average)

Q1 Edward IV's father and which other close relative were killed at the Battle of Wakefield?

Q2 Who was Edward IV's wife?

Q3 How many times did Edward IV serve as King of England?

Q4 Edward IV was the first English king from which royal house?

Q5 Which brother did Edward IV have executed?

Q6 Which Lancastrian heir to the English throne was killed at the Battle of Tewkesbury?

Q7 In what year was Edward IV's heir, the future Edward V, born?

Q8 Which nobleman played a key role in installing Edward IV on the English throne, but later turned against him?

Q9 In what county did the Battle of Mortimer's Cross take place?

Q10 Where was Edward IV born?

Edward V (average)

Q1 What was the name of Edward V's younger brother?

Q2 In what year did Edward V briefly reign?

Q3 What position did the future Richard III hold during Edward V's reign?

Q4 Before becoming king, where was Edward V's court based?

Q5 Edward V was declared illegitimate in which Act of Parliament?

Q6 Where was Edward V and his brother held after his deposition?

Q7 Where was Edward V born?

Q8 Who was in charge of Edward V's upbringing?

Q9 Which physician attended to Edward V?

Q10 Which Tudor historian claimed Edward V and his brother were murdered at midnight on Richard III's orders?

Richard III (easy)

Q1 Who was Richard III defeated by at the Battle of Bosworth Field?

A Henry VI
B Henry VII
C Edward IV
D Edward V

Q2 Before becoming king, Richard III was the Duke of what?

A Edinburgh
B York
C Kent
D Gloucester

Q3 Richard III was the final English king from which royal house?

A Lancaster
B York
C Tudor
D Windsor

Q4 Where is Richard III buried?

A York Minster
B Westminster Abbey
C Leicester Cathedral
D Salisbury Cathedral

Q5 What relation were the Princes in the Tower to Richard III?

A Sons
B Cousins
C Brothers
D Nephews

Q6 What was the name of the Tudor historian who wrote *The History of King Richard the Third*?

A Thomas More
B Thomas Cromwell
C Dominic Mancini
D Desiderius Erasmus

Q7 Which county is Richard III most commonly associated with?

A Rutland
B Shropshire
C Herefordshire
D Yorkshire

Q8 What was Richard III's religion?

A Catholic
B Protestant
C Orthodox
D Presbyterian

Q9 In what year did Richard III become King of England?

A 1470
B 1483
C 1485
D 1490

Q10 Richard III is the main protagonist in which William Shakespeare play?

A *The Princes in the Tower*
B *Bosworth*
C *Richard III*
D *Tudor*

Richard III (average)

Q1 In what year was the Battle of Bosworth fought?

Q2 What was Richard III's personal badge?

Q3 What was the name of Richard III's legitimate son?

Q4 Richard III's wife was a daughter of which nobleman?

Q5 Who led an unsuccessful rebellion against Richard III in the autumn of 1483?

Q6 Who did Richard III depose to become King of England?

Q7 Richard III's demise marked the end of which protracted conflict?

Q8 How many of Richard III's brothers served as King of England?

Q9 Which Archbishop of Canterbury crowned Richard III King of England?

Q10 In what year was Richard III's first and only parliament held?

Richard III (expert)

Q1 Which university played an instrumental role in the discovery of Richard III's body?

Q2 In what town did Richard III have Anthony Woodville, Earl Rivers (amongst other members of Edward V's household) arrested?

Q3 Which 1484 Act of Parliament legitimised Richard III's claim to the throne?

Q4 Which powerful nobleman was hastily executed after a meeting of the royal council at the Tower of London on 13 June 1483?

Q5 Which bishop provided evidence that led to Edward IV and Elizabeth Woodville's marriage to be declared bigamous?

Q6 Which nobleman's intervention at the Battle of Bosworth ultimately led to Richard III's defeat?

Q7 William Collingbourne's famous lampoon 'The Catte, the Ratte and Lovell our dogge rulyth all Englande under a hogge' attacked Richard III and three of his supporters. Who were they?

Q8 During his adolescence, Richard III developed what condition?

Q9 When Edward IV died, what did Richard III become?

Q10 Who was Richard III's main rival in the north of England?

Henry VII (average)

Q1 Who was Henry VII's mother?

Q2 Which king did Henry VII defeat at Bosworth Field?

Q3 Which castle was Henry VII born at?

Q4 Henry VII founded which royal dynasty?

Q5 From which country did Henry VII descend?

Q6 Who pretended to be Edward Plantagenet, Earl of Warwick in 1487?

Q7 Perkin Warbeck was born in which present-day country?

Q8 Who was Henry VII's oldest legitimate son?

Q9 Who did Henry VII marry to unite the Houses of Lancaster and York, ultimately bringing an end to the Wars of the Roses?

Q10 What relation was Jasper Tudor to Henry VII?

Henry VIII (easy)

Q1 How many wives did Henry VIII have?

A 1
B 2
C 4
D 6

Q2 Henry VIII changed England's state religion to what?

A Catholicism
B Orthodoxy
C Protestantism
D Judaism

Q3 In the early stages of his reign, Henry VIII was referred to as the 'Defender of the' what?

A Faith
B Kingdom
C Crown
D People

Q4 How many of Henry VIII's children went on to rule England?

A 0
B 1
C 2
D 3

Q5 The Dissolution of the what occurred from 1536 onwards?

A Parliament
B Monasteries
C Clergy
D Council

Q6 Which kingdom did Henry VIII fight against at the Battle of the Spurs?

A Kingdom of Spain
B Kingdom of the Netherlands
C Kingdom of Bulgaria
D Kingdom of France

Q7 Henry's will designated how many executors to serve on a council of regency until Edward VI reached the age of 18?

A 1
B 5
C 10
D 16

Q8 Which monarch, over 100 years after Henry VIII's death, was buried in the same vault?

A Elizabeth I of England
B James I of England
C Charles I of England
D Charles II of England

Q9 The Rough Wooing was a war between the Kingdom of England and which other kingdom?

A Kingdom of Ireland
B Kingdom of Spain
C Kingdom of Scotland
D Kingdom of France

Q10 What was the *Mary Rose*?

A Crown
B Chapel
C Relic
D Ship

Henry VIII (average)

Q1 Which of Henry VIII's wives is buried alongside him in St. George's chapel in Windsor Castle?

Q2 Which of Henry VIII's wives were executed?

Q3 Which position did Henry VIII create and appoint himself to in the Church of England?

Q4 Which author and statesman was executed in 1535?

Q5 The Crown of Ireland Act 1542 created what title?

Q6 Who were Catherine of Aragon's parents?

Q7 Which pope refused to annul Henry VIII's marriage to Catherine of Aragon?

Q8 In which palace did Henry VIII die?

Q9 What method of execution was used for the wives Henry VIII condemned to death?

Q10 In what year did Henry VIII become King of England?

Henry VIII (expert)

Q1 Under which acts were England and Wales legally unified?

Q2 In what year was the Royal Navy founded?

Q3 Which wife was Henry VIII married to the longest?

Q4 What was the name of Henry VIII's first son?

Q5 The Treaty of London (1518) was what kind of pact?

Q6 What theological treatise did Henry VIII publish in 1521?

Q7 Mark Smeaton was executed for committing adultery with who?

Q8 Thomas Cromwell served as Governor of which island?

Q9 The Treasons Act 1534 made it treason to do what?

Q10 Who baptised Henry VIII?

Edward VI (average)

Q1 Who was Edward VI's mother?

Q2 Edward VI was a devout follower of which form of Christianity?

Q3 Which noble was educated at Henry VIII's court and became a close friend of Edward VI?

Q4 Edward VI appears in which Mark Twain novel?

Q5 How was Lady Jane Grey related to Edward VI?

Q6 Who dominated politics in the early stages of Edward VI's reign?

Q7 How old was Edward VI when he died?

Q8 Who did the Kingdom of England fight at the Battle of Pinkie Cleugh?

Q9 Where was Edward VI born?

Q10 Henry VIII's will named how many executors, who were to act as Edward's Council until he reached the age of eighteen?

Mary I (average)

Q1 Mary I was an ardent supporter of what church?

Q2 Who was Mary I's husband?

Q3 Who was Mary I's mother?

Q4 What nickname is commonly given to Mary I?

Q5 Who was briefly proclaimed Queen of England after the death of Edward VI?

Q6 How many children did Mary I have?

Q7 Which powerful nobleman was executed on 22 August 1553?

Q8 What was the name of the popular uprising that occurred in 1554?

Q9 Which Archbishop of Canterbury was executed during Mary I's reign?

Q10 The Siege of Calais occurred in what year?

Elizabeth I (easy)

Q1 Elizabeth I was the last English monarch from what royal house?

A Plantagenet
B Tudor
C Stuart
D Orange-Nassau

Q2 Who was Elizabeth I's mother?

A Catherine of Aragon
B Anne of Cleves
C Catherine Parr
D Anne Boleyn

Q3 England was converted back to what religion during Elizabeth I's reign?

A Catholicism
B Orthodoxy
C Lollardism
D Protestantism

Q4 Which conflict occurred between 1585 and 1604?

A Anglo-Spanish War
B Anglo-Dutch War
C Thirty Years' War
D War of the Austrian Succession

Q5 How many ships were there in the Spanish Armada?

A 15
B 50
C 130
D 300

Q6 How many times did Elizabeth I marry?

A 0
B 1
C 2
D 3

Q7 What was Francis Drake's occupation?

A Executioner
B Academic
C Advisor
D Privateer

Q8 The ruler of which kingdom succeeded Elizabeth I?

A Kingdom of France
B Kingdom of Bohemia
C Kingdom of Scotland
D Kingdom of Denmark

Q9 Simon Renard was an ambassador serving what kingdom?

A Kingdom of Spain
B Kingdom of England
C Kingdom of France
D Kingdom of Portugal

Q10 Elizabeth I's favourite, Robert Dudley, was Earl of what?

A Rutland
B Wessex
C Leicester
D Northumberland

Elizabeth I (average)

Q1 In her later years, what did Elizabeth I refuse to have in any of her rooms?

Q2 Name one of Elizabeth I's nicknames.

Q3 Who was Elizabeth I's chief advisor for the majority of her reign?

Q4 Elizabeth I was responsible for the execution of which Scottish monarch?

Q5 In what year was the Spanish Armada defeated?

Q6 Which world-renowned playwright rose to prominence during Elizabeth I's reign?

Q7 Francis Drake famously captained which galleon?

Q8 Ingram Frizer is well-known for reportedly killing who?

Q9 Elizabeth I courted which Duke of Anjou?

Q10 In which palace did Elizabeth I die?

Elizabeth I (expert)

Q1 The Act of Supremacy 1558 replaced which act that had been passed by Henry VIII and repealed by Mary I?

Q2 Who commanded the Spanish Armada?

Q3 What was Christopher Marlowe's occupation?

Q4 Who was Elizabeth I's first governess?

Q5 Katherine Champernowne was known by what name to Elizabeth I?

Q6 Which 1543 act was revoked in Edward VI's will?

Q7 How old was Elizabeth I when she became Queen of England?

Q8 Who crowned Elizabeth I Queen of England?

Q9 How were Elizabeth I and Mary, Queen of Scots related?

Q10 Which Moroccan ambassador visited England in 1600?

James I (easy)

Q1 Who was the leader of the Gunpowder Plot?

A Guy Fawkes
B Robert Catesby
C Thomas Percy
D Robert Keyes

Q2 Before becoming King of England, what other kingdom was James I king of?

A France
B The Netherlands
C Scotland
D Sweden

Q3 James I was the first English king from which royal house?

A Plantagenet
B Tudor
C Stuart
D Hanover

Q4 In what year was the *King James Bible* published

A 1605
B 1611
C 1615
D 1620

Q5 In what year did James I become King of England?

A 1583
B 1590
C 1603
D 1605

Q6 How old was James I when he first became a king?

A 1
B 5
C 18
D 23

Q7 What was the name of James I's wife?

A Marie Antoinette
B Eleanor of Aquitaine
C Margaret of Anjou
D Anne of Denmark

Q8 What caused the death of James I's father, Henry Stuart, Lord Darnley?

A Smallpox
B Murder
C Heart attack
D Starvation

Q9 Where was James I born?

A Tower of London
B Stirling Castle
C Conwy Castle
D Edinburgh Castle

Q10 Robert Cecil served as Secretary of what between 1596 and 1612?

A Defence
B State
C Treasury
D Colonial Affairs

James I (average)

Q1 Who was James I's mother?

Q2 What name is given to the era when James I was King of England?

Q3 What did James I want to do to the English and Scottish Parliaments?

Q4 The English colonisation of where commenced during James I's reign?

Q5 On what date in 1605 did the Gunpowder Plot occur?

Q6 Who was James I's eldest son?

Q7 What was the name of the Duke of Buckingham, the favourite and alleged lover of James I?

Q8 Sir Walter Raleigh was executed in what year of James I's reign?

Q9 How was Guy Fawkes executed?

Q10 Which major European war took place during James I's reign?

James I (expert)

Q1 James I was the great-great-grandson of which king?

Q2 What was the name of the philosophical dissertation that James I published in 1597?

Q3 James Hamilton assassinated which Regent of Scotland before James I came into his majority?

Q4 The Main Plot was an alleged conspiracy to replace James I with who?

Q5 The Gentleman Adventurers of Fife were awarded lands on what island by James I?

Q6 The Addled Parliament took place in what year?

Q7 What was the occupation of Inigo Jones?

Q8 In what year was the Globe Theatre destroyed by a fire?

Q9 The Millenary Petition was a list of requests given to James I by who?

Q10 What began in Ulster during the reign of James I?

Charles I (easy)

Q1 What conflict took place during Charles I's reign?

A The Anarchy
B The English Civil War
C The Wars of the Roses
D The American Revolution

Q2 In what country was Charles I born?

A England
B Ireland
C Scotland
D France

Q3 How many of Charles I's children went on to become King of England?

A 0
B 1
C 2
D 3

Q4 In what year was Charles I executed?

A 1630
B 1649
C 1660
D 1672

Q5 Who governed England after Charles I's execution?

A Charles II
B Queen Henrietta Maria
C Thomas Fairfax
D Oliver Cromwell

Q6 Who was the Parliamentary commander-in-chief?

A Oliver Cromwell
B John Pym
C John Hampden
D Thomas Fairfax

Q7 In what castle was Charles I imprisoned?

A Carisbrooke Castle
B Nottingham Castle
C Pontefract Castle
D Balmoral Castle

Q8 The Wars of the Three Kingdoms took place in which kingdoms?

A England, Scotland and France
B England, Scotland and Spain
C England, Scotland and Ireland
D England, Ireland and France

Q9 The Grand Remonstrance was a list of grievances presented to Charles I by who?

A His wife
B His sons
C The pope
D The English Parliament

Q10 How was Charles I executed?

A Beheaded
B Hung
C Boiled
D Burned

Charles I (average)

Q1 What was the name of Charles I's wife?

Q2 The Roundheads were supporters of who during the English Civil War?

Q3 By what name was the Kingdom of England referred to between 1649 and 1660?

Q4 Charles I was executed outside which palace?

Q5 What was the name of the army that was created by the Parliamentarians during the English Civil War?

Q6 The period from 1629 to 1640 is known by what name?

Q7 On what charge was Charles I executed?

Q8 The Battle of Marston Moor was fought in what county?

Q9 Apart from Charles I, who was the most prominent royalist leader in the English Civil War?

Q10 Who was Charles I's youngest son?

Charles I (expert)

Q1 Charles I raised his army in the English Civil War by using what medieval method?

Q2 Charles I was a staunch supporter of what political and religious doctrine of royal and political legitimacy?

Q3 Which Archbishop of Canterbury was executed in 1645?

Q4 In which pub was George Villiers, Duke of Buckingham assassinated?

Q5 Who were the 'Five Members' from the House of Commons who Charles I attempted to have arrested in 1642?

Q6 Between 1642 and 1651 how many English Civil Wars were there?

Q7 The Bishops' Wars of 1639 and 1640 were fought between Scottish Royalists and who else?

Q8 *Charles I in Three Positions* is a painting of Charles I by which Flemish artist?

Q9 John Hampden was mortally wounded during which battle?

Q10 Pride's Purge preceded which parliament?

Charles II (average)

Q1 The Popish Plot was a fictitious conspiracy concocted by who?

Q2 What is the period called between Charles I's execution and Charles II's rise to power?

Q3 In what year did the Restoration begin?

Q4 Who defeated Charles II at the Battle of Worcester?

Q5 How was Moll Davis associated with Charles II?

Q6 The Cavalier Parliament endured just under how many years?

Q7 The Rye House Plot of 1683 was a plot to do what?

Q8 Charles II was known as the Merry what?

Q9 How many children did Charles II have with his wife Catherine of Braganza?

Q10 Charles II accompanied his father to which 1642 battle?

James II (average)

Q1 James II was deposed in what revolution?

Q2 James II was the last king of what faith to rule England?

Q3 The birth of which prince precipitated James II's downfall?

Q4 Before James II, how many other Stuart monarchs had been deposed in England?

Q5 Which political movement aimed to restore James II and his heirs to the English throne?

Q6 In what country did James II die?

Q7 Which king did James II fight at the Battle of the Boyne?

Q8 Which king offered James II asylum?

Q9 The Seven Bishops were imprisoned for their opposition to what proclamations made by James II?

Q10 How was James II related to his predecessor, Charles II?

William III and Mary II (average)

Q1 William III was better known by what name?

Q2 In what republic was William III born?

Q3 Who was Mary II's father?

Q4 What religion did both William III and Mary II adhere to?

Q5 Did William III or Mary II reign longer?

Q6 In what palace did both William III and Mary II die?

Q7 The Bill of Rights was passed in what year?

Q8 The seven English noblemen who wrote to William III, inviting him to invade England, were later named what?

Q9 Henry Compton, who crowned William III and Mary II King and Queen of England, held what position in the church?

Q10 Who composed *Music for the Funeral of Queen Mary*?

Anne (easy)

Q1 Anne was the first Queen of what?

A England
B Great Britain
C Ireland
D Isle of Mann

Q2 Where is Anne buried?

A St Paul's Cathedral
B Windsor Castle
C York Minster
D Westminster Abbey

Q3 What church was Anne a member of?

A Catholic
B Orthodox
C Presbyterian
D Church of England

Q4 What royal house was Anne a member of?

A Plantagenet
B Tudor
C Stuart
D Windsor

Q5 Who was Anne's only child to survive infancy?

A Prince William, Duke of Gloucester
B Prince Richard, Duke of York
C Edward, Prince of Wales
D James, Earl of Shrewsbury

Q6 In what year was Anne's coronation?

A 1700
B 1702
C 1707
D 1710

Q7 Which party gained a majority in the House of Commons in the 1708 general election?

A Whig
B Liberal
C Tory
D Labour

Q8 What war took place during Anne's reign?

A Crimean War
B War of the Spanish Succession
C Napoleonic Wars
D Seven Years' War

Q9 Who instigated an uprising in 1715?

A Jacobites
B Puritans
C Luddites
D Socialists

Q10 In what year did Anne first fall pregnant?

A 1675
B 1680
C 1684
D 1700

Anne (average)

Q1 Which palace was Anne born in?

Q2 Which political party did Anne favour?

Q3 In what years were the two Acts of Union passed?

Q4 How was Anne related to Mary II?

Q5 Anne's husband, Prince George, was from what country?

Q6 Immediately following her marriage, where did Anne and her husband reside?

Q7 Shortly after her accession, what position did Anne appoint her husband to?

Q8 The 'Great Storm' struck southern England in which year of Anne's reign?

Q9 Which traditional religious practice did Anne reinstitute?

Q10 How were Anne and her successor, George I, related?

Anne (expert)

Q1 Sarah Churchill, an estranged friend of Anne, held which title?

Q2 Anne's mother, Anne Hyde, was the first wife of who?

Q3 As a child, Anne suffered from a medical condition affecting which part of the body?

Q4 Prince William, Duke of Gloucester was how old when he died?

Q5 How many times did Anne fall pregnant?

Q6 At the start of Anne's reign, what position in government did Robert Harley hold?

Q7 What name was given to the group of Whig politicians who were seen to direct the management of the Whig Party during the reigns of William III and Anne?

Q8 John Somers held which political office between 1708 and 1710?

Q9 Who was Archbishop of Canterbury during Anne's reign?

Q10 In what year did Anne become Princess Anne of Denmark?

George I (easy)

Q1 What was George I's primary title before he became King of Great Britain?

A Pope
B Elector of Hanover
C Holy Roman Emperor
D Earl of Northumberland

Q2 Who became Britain's first de facto prime minister during George I's reign?

A Winston Churchill
B William Pitt the Elder
C William Gladstone
D Robert Walpole

Q3 How many wives did George I have?

A 0
B 1
C 2
D 3

Q4 The Jacobite, John Erskine, was from what country?

A England
B Ireland
C Wales
D Scotland

Q5 For what main reason was George I disliked by the British?

A He was Catholic
B He was authoritarian
C He was German
D He was greedy

Q6 George I was a great grandson of which English monarch?

A James I
B James II
C Charles I
D Charles II

Q7 How many members of the House of Hanover ruled Great Britain?

A 1
B 4
C 6
D 9

Q8 The War of the Quadruple Alliance pitted a coalition of countries (Britain, France, the Holy Roman Empire and the Dutch Republic) against which kingdom?

A Portugal
B Spain
C Bulgaria
D Russia

Q9 As well as being his wife, what relation was Sophia Dorothea of Celle to George I?

A Sister
B Cousin
C Second Cousin
D Stepmother

Q10 During George I's reign, who was the main Catholic claimant to the throne of Great Britain?

A James II of England
B Henry Benedict Stuart
C Mary of Modena
D James Francis Edward Stuart

George I (average)

Q1 What political party did the first British Prime Minister belong to?

Q2 What royal house did George I belong to?

Q3 George I served at the Battle of Vienna during which war?

Q4 Melusine von der Schulenburg was associated with George I in what way?

Q5 What occurred alongside George I's coronation in over 20 English towns?

Q6 In which stately home did George I have his wife, Sophia Dorothea of Celle, imprisoned?

Q7 What was the main difference between governing Britain and governing Hanover?

Q8 Which 1701 Act of Parliament ultimately led to George I becoming King of Great Britain?

Q9 What did George I die from?

Q10 What branch of Christianity did George I adhere to?

George I (expert)

Q1 In what city did George I die?

Q2 How old was George I when he ascended the British throne?

Q3 Who did George I's wife, Sophia Dorothea of Celle, allegedly have an affair with?

Q4 In 1717 George I contributed to the establishment of which anti-Spanish league?

Q5 In which chapel was George I initially buried?

Q6 Which nobleman led the 1715 Jacobite uprising?

Q7 The Septennial Act 1716 increased the maximum length of a parliament from 3 years to how many?

Q8 Who did George I refuse to have as regent of Great Britain when, on a number of occasions, he returned to Hanover?

Q9 What was George I's father's name?

Q10 What was George I's middle name?

George II (easy)

Q1 How was George II's successor, George III, related to him?

A Son
B Grandson
C Nephew
D Brother

Q2 Both of George II's parents committed what sin?

A Murder
B Charlatanism
C Adultery
D Blasphemy

Q3 How old was George II when he became King of Great Britain?

A 9
B 23
C 43
D 62

Q4 *Music for the Royal Fireworks* was composed to celebrate the end of which war?

A The War of Austrian Succession
B The War of Spanish Succession
C Seven Years' War
D Crimean War

Q5 George II is the most recent British monarch to be buried where?

A Windsor Castle
B Westminster Abbey
C St Paul's Cathedral
D Sandringham Estate

Q6 George II donated the royal library to which museum in 1757?

A British Museum
B Natural History Museum
C The National Gallery
D German Historical Museum

Q7 In which major film franchise does George II make an appearance?

A *Lord of the Rings*
B *Harry Potter*
C *The Mummy*
D *Pirates of the Caribbean*

Q8 How many times did George II marry?

A 0
B 1
C 2
D 3

Q9 What was George II's full name?

A George Frederick
B George James
C George Augustus
D George Wilhelm

Q10 George II held what position in the Holy Roman Empire?

A Prince-elector
B King
C Prime minister
D Bishop

George II (average)

Q1 George II was the last British monarch to be born where?

Q2 The last Jacobite rebellion took place in which year of George II's reign?

Q3 Until the age of four, what was the only language George II knew how to speak?

Q4 George II famously had a poor relationship with which relative?

Q5 What was the name of George II's eldest son?

Q6 After his defeat at the Battle of Culloden, Charles Edward Stuart disguised himself as a maid called what?

Q7 In what year did the Seven Years' War break out?

Q8 What was significant about George II dying at the age of 76?

Q9 George II founded the first university in the Electorate of Hanover. What was its name?

Q10 Before he died, George II left instructions for what to be done to his and his wife's coffins?

George II (expert)

Q1 George II became the last British monarch to lead his troops in which battle?

Q2 In which palace did George II die?

Q3 In which 1705 Act of Parliament was George II naturalised as an English subject?

Q4 Which composer composed *Zadok the Priest* for George II's coronation?

Q5 The Annus Mirabilis of 1759 refers to what?

Q6 In what year of George II's reign did the French plan to invade Britain?

Q7 A post-mortem revealed George II had died as a result of what?

Q8 George II served as the chancellor of which college?

Q9 A statue of George II by the Flemish sculptor John Van Nost stands in which London square?

Q10 Which asteroid was named after George II?

George III (easy)

Q1 In what year did the acts come into force that united the Kingdom of Great Britain and the Kingdom of Ireland?

A 1790
B 1795
C 1801
D 1809

Q2 George III assumed which title in Hanover in 1814?

A Prince of Hanover
B Elector of Hanover
C Emperor of Hanover
D King of Hanover

Q3 Unlike his two predecessors what was George III's first language?

A English
B German
C French
D Latin

Q4 Key colonies on which continent were lost during George III's reign?

A Asia
B Africa
C North America
D South America

Q5 How many children did George III and his wife have?

A 0
B 1
C 3
D 15

Q6 William Pitt the Elder acquired which title from George III?

A Duke of York
B Earl of Chatham
C Earl of Wessex
D Prince of Wales

Q7 The Intolerable Acts were passed following which event?

A Declaration of Independence
B Battle of Trafalgar
C Siege of Yorktown
D Boston Tea Party

Q8 The Gordon Riots of 1780 were based on what sentiments?

A Pro-democracy
B Pro-royalty
C Anti-Catholic
D Anti-Puritan

Q9 How many Pitts served as Prime Minister during George III's reign?

A 0
B 1
C 2
D 3

Q10 Who attempted to assassinate George III in 1800?

A John Wilkes Booth
B Lee Harvey Oswald
C James Hadfield
D James Earl Ray

George III (average)

Q1 How many times did George III visit Hanover?

Q2 Which European ruler threatened to invade Britain during George III's reign?

Q3 In the latter part of his life, George III suffered from what kind of illness?

Q4 Who ruled as George III's proxy during the Regency era?

Q5 After whose death was the future George III created Prince of Wales?

Q6 The King's Library, assembled by George III, was one of the most important collections of books and pamphlets of which intellectual and philosophical movement?

Q7 Who successfully persuaded George III not to marry Lady Sarah Lennox?

Q8 The Royal Proclamation of 1763 restricted the westward expansion of what?

Q9 'No taxation without representation' was a key grievance of citizens of which group of colonies?

Q10 Who was the first United States Ambassador to the United Kingdom?

George III (expert)

Q1 In which house was George III born?

Q2 At the age of 10, George III took part in a family production of which Joseph Addison play?

Q3 In what duchy was George III's wife born?

Q4 Who served as the first Scottish Prime Minister of Great Britain between 1762 and 1763?

Q5 The radical newspaper *The North Briton* is associated with which Member of Parliament?

Q6 Which Prime Minister led Britain through the majority of the American Revolutionary War?

Q7 The Royal Marriages Act 1772 was repealed as a result of which 2011 agreement?

Q8 George III allegedly shook hands with a tree, mistakenly believing it to be who?

Q9 Which Lincolnshire physician is known for treating George III?

Q10 The Ministry of All the Talents was a government of national unity formed by which Prime Minister?

George IV (average)

Q1 What did George IV commission John Nash to build in Brighton?

Q2 How many years did George IV's reign last?

Q3 What was the name of George IV's wife?

Q4 How was George IV related to his successor, William IV?

Q5 The Pains and Penalties Bill was introduced to Parliament in 1820 at the request of George IV in an attempt to do what?

Q6 How many legitimate children did George IV have?

Q7 Which chapel at Windsor Castle is George IV buried in?

Q8 George IV was baptised by which Archbishop of Canterbury?

Q9 In 1821 George IV became the first monarch to pay a state visit to which country since Richard II?

Q10 Which party governed Britain during George IV's reign?

William IV (average)

Q1 Which palace was William IV born in?

Q2 Owing to his service in the Royal Navy, what was William IV nicknamed?

Q3 How many illegitimate children did William IV have with the actress Dorothea Jordan?

Q4 What important act concerning slavery was passed during William IV's reign?

Q5 What relation was the future Queen Victoria to William IV?

Q6 What rank did William IV enter the Royal Navy at when he was thirteen years old?

Q7 Why did William IV attempt to marry Catherine Tylney-Long?

Q8 William IV supported which country's independence?

Q9 Who acted as viceroy of Hanover during William IV's reign?

Q10 The Reform Act 1832 introduced wide-ranging changes to what?

Victoria (easy)

Q1 Queen Victoria was the last British monarch from which royal house?

A Plantagenet
B Tudor
C Stuart
D Hanover

Q2 Queen Victoria wore black for the remainder of her life after the death of which relative?

A Sister
B Mother
C Son
D Husband

Q3 How many people served as Prime Minister during Queen Victoria's reign?

A 2
B 4
C 10
D 17

Q4 Queen Victoria was nicknamed the 'grandmother' of what?

A England
B Queens
C Europe
D George

Q5 How many attempts were there to assassinate Queen Victoria?

A 0
B 1
C 3
D 8

Q6 What did Ireland suffer from between 1845 and 1849?

A Great Famine
B Black Death
C Revolution
D Mass unemployment

Q7 Which controversial law(s) were repealed in 1846?

A Poor Laws
B Corn Laws
C Treaty of Union
D Titulus Regius

Q8 How many political parties governed Britain during Queen Victoria's reign?

A 1
B 2
C 3
D 4

Q9 John Brown, a personal attendant and favourite of Queen Victoria, was from what country?

A England
B Germany
C Ireland
D Scotland

Q10 The Victoria Cross was introduced in 1856 to reward acts of valour during which war?

A Crimean War
B Anglo-Zulu War
C First Boer War
D First World War

Victoria (average)

Q1 What additional title did Queen Victoria adopt in 1876?

Q2 Which island did Queen Victoria die on?

Q3 What was the name of Queen Victoria's husband?

Q4 At the time of her birth, what place was Queen Victoria in the line of succession?

Q5 Who was Prime Minister at the time of Queen Victoria's coronation?

Q6 Whose death in 1839 gave Queen Victoria a negative image?

Q7 Who was Queen Victoria's childhood governess?

Q8 Queen Victoria's youngest son, Leopold, was affected by what disease?

Q9 Which Prime Minister did Queen Victoria have a better relationship with: Benjamin Disraeli or William Gladstone?

Q10 Which joint-stock company was dissolved after the Indian Rebellion of 1857?

Victoria (expert)

Q1 How old was Queen Victoria when she inherited the throne?

Q2 How many children did Queen Victoria have?

Q3 Under what set of rules was Queen Victoria raised?

Q4 What was the name of the King Charles Spaniel owned by Queen Victoria during her youth?

Q5 Who became King of Hanover after the death of William IV?

Q6 Approximately how many visitors came to London for Queen Victoria's coronation celebrations?

Q7 Who attempted to assassinate Queen Victoria in 1840?

Q8 In what year was the Anti-Corn Law League founded?

Q9 Whose attempt to assassinate Napoleon III ultimately resulted in Lord Palmerston resigning as Prime Minister?

Q10 Why did Roderick Maclean shoot at Queen Victoria as her carriage left Windsor railway station in 1882?

Edward VII (average)

Q1 Edward VII played a part in the modernisation of which Royal Navy fleet?

Q2 Which war was Britain engaged in when Edward VII came to power?

Q3 What name has been given to the era when Edward VII was king?

Q4 Edward VII famously had a poor relationship with which nephew?

Q5 The constitutional crisis Edward VII died in the midst of was resolved by which Act of Parliament?

Q6 The 1909/1910 People's Budget was proposed by which political party?

Q7 Which country was Edward VII's wife born in?

Q8 Where was Edward VII born, and where did he die?

Q9 Edward VII was the first British king from which royal house?

Q10 What caused Edward VII's coronation to be delayed?

George V (average)

Q1 Which governess cared for George V's sickly son, Prince John?

Q2 At the start of George V's reign the Parliament Act 1911 established the supremacy of which House of Parliament?

Q3 Which cadet training ship did George V join when he was 12 years old?

Q4 In 1917 what name did George V change his royal house to?

Q4 What was George V's wife called?

Q6 The Commonwealth was originally created through which 1926 declaration?

Q7 In what year did Ramsay MacDonald become the first Labour Prime Minister?

Q8 George V ultimately opposed a government plan to offer which European ruler and his family asylum in 1917?

Q9 In what year did George V make the first royal Christmas speech on the radio?

Q10 George V ordered a portrait of himself by which artist to be burned?

Edward VIII (average)

Q1 In what year did Edward VIII serve as King of the United Kingdom?

Q2 On which birthday was the future Edward VIII named Prince of Wales?

Q3 What was the name of the woman Edward VIII abdicated in order to marry?

Q4 In what country did Edward VIII die?

Q5 What title did Edward VIII obtain after his abdication?

Q6 Who did Edward VIII meet, against the advice of the British government, in 1937?

Q7 Field Marshal Horatio Herbert Kitchener refused to allow the future Edward VIII to do what in the First World War?

Q8 Operation Willi refers to an unsuccessful attempt by the German SS to do what?

Q9 In which town is Edward VIII buried?

Q10 Edward VIII had a love affair with which Parisian during the First World War?

George VI (average)

Q1 George VI led the United Kingdom through which war?

Q2 George VI was the first head of what and the last emperor of what?

Q3 What name was George VI known by before his accession?

Q4 After George VI's death, what did people start calling his wife, Elizabeth Angela Marguerite Bowes-Lyon, to avoid confusion?

Q5 In the mid-1920s George VI had what kind of therapy?

Q6 Who was George VI's partner in the 1926 Wimbledon Men's Doubles tournament?

Q7 Which brother of George VI was killed in active service in 1942?

Q8 Who was George VI's preferred choice to replace Neville Chamberlain as Prime Minister?

Q9 George VI addressed which intergovernmental organisation in its first assembly in 1946?

Q10 Who played George VI in the 2010 film *The King's Speech*?

Elizabeth II (average)

Q1 Which service did Elizabeth II serve in during the Second World War?

Q2 How many Commonwealth realms is Elizabeth II queen of?

Q3 In 2017 Elizabeth II became the first British monarch to reach which jubilee?

Q4 Which former daughter-in-law of Elizabeth II was killed in a car crash in Paris in 1997?

Q5 Who was Prime Minister when Elizabeth II came to power?

Q6 Who is Elizabeth II's husband?

Q7 Who was Elizabeth II's only sibling?

Q8 Who was Archbishop of Canterbury when Elizabeth II came to power?

Q9 Elizabeth II holds what position in the Church of England?

Q10 In 1983 Elizabeth II was angered when US President Ronald Reagan ordered the invasion of what country?

Answers

Alfred the Great (easy)

Q1 Wessex
Q2 Great Heathen Army
Q3 Guthrum
Q4 The Anglo-Saxons
Q5 Asser
Q6 Winchester
Q7 1
Q8 Hyde Abbey
Q9 Rome
Q10 Son

Alfred the Great (average)

Q1 Æthelwulf, King of Wessex
Q2 Mercia
Q3 3
Q4 Christianity
Q5 Osburh
Q6 Ealhswith
Q7 Viking invasion
Q8 Laws
Q9 English
Q10 Learning/Education

Alfred the Great (expert)

Q1 871
Q2 Anglo-Saxon document
Q3 Military road
Q4 *Pastoral Care*
Q5 12th
Q6 Somerset
Q7 899
Q8 Æthelflæd, Lady of the Mercians
Q9 Carolingian Renaissance
Q10 Drake-class armoured cruiser

Edward the Elder (easy)

Q1 Father
Q2 3
Q3 House of Wessex
Q4 King of the Anglo-Saxons
Q5 Kingston upon Thames
Q6 899
Q7 Battle of Tettenhall
Q8 3
Q9 Cheshire
Q10 Edward the Martyr

Edward the Elder (average)

Q1 His cousin, Æthelwold
Q2 Kingship
Q3 Oswald of Northumbria
Q4 Archbishop of Canterbury
Q5 New Minster
Q6 Wife
Q7 Lady of the Mercians
Q8 Warfare
Q9 893
Q10 9th

Edward the Elder (expert)

Q1 899-924
Q2 902
Q3 Ecgwynn
Q4 870s
Q5 A hillfort
Q6 Mercia
Q7 Eadgyth
Q8 Æthelred
Q9 Bishop of Winchester
Q10 Grimbald

Æthelstan (average)

Q1 England
Q2 Scotland
Q3 Battle of Brunanburh
Q4 Viking York
Q5 Malmesbury Abbey
Q6 Half brother
Q7 Wales
Q8 Æthelstan A
Q9 Scholar
Q10 Old English

Edmund I (average)

Q1 Grandson
Q2 Mass
Q3 2
Q4 Godfather
Q5 Strathclyde
Q6 Louis IV of France
Q7 Pucklechurch
Q8 Otto I, Holy Roman Emperor
Q9 Brother
Q10 Kingston upon Thames

Eadred (average)

Q1 Nephew
Q2 0
Q3 Oda of Canterbury
Q4 Kingdom of Northumbria
Q5 Digestive illness
Q6 Northumbria
Q7 Winchester Cathedral
Q8 946-955
Q9 Kingston upon Thames
Q10 Eadgifu of Kent

Eadwig (average)

Q1 All-Fair
Q2 15
Q3 Ælfgifu of Shaftesbury
Q4 Frances Burney
Q5 Dunstan
Q6 Ælfgifu
Q7 Gloucester
Q8 River Thames
Q9 To flirt with two women
Q10 959

Edgar (average)

Q1 The Peaceful
Q2 Edmund I
Q3 Archbishop of Canterbury
Q4 Bath
Q5 Æthelwald, Ealdorman of East Anglia
Q6 Longparish, Hampshire
Q7 Chester
Q8 Glastonbury Abbey
Q9 House of Wessex
Q10 Dunstan

Edward the Martyr (average)

Q1 Æthelred the Unready
Q2 Corfe Castle
Q3 He was an illegitimate child
Q4 Dunstan of Canterbury and Oswald of Worcester
Q5 Murder
Q6 Anglican Communion, Catholic Church, Eastern Orthodox Church
Q7 March 18
Q8 St. Edward the Martyr Orthodox Church
Q9 975-78
Q10 Ealdorman of Mercia

Æthelred the Unready (average)

Q1 2
Q2 Well-advised
Q3 991
Q4 Danegeld
Q5 Danes
Q6 Sweyn Forkbeard
Q7 Henry III
Q8 Emma of Normandy
Q9 Sweyn Forkbeard
Q10 London

Sweyn Forkbeard (average)

Q1 1013-14
Q2 Harald Bluetooth
Q3 Denmark
Q4 Æthelred the Unready
Q5 Baltic Sea
Q6 St. Brice's Day massacre
Q7 Cnut the Great
Q8 House of Knýtlinga
Q9 Eric the Victorious, King of Sweden
Q10 Normandy

Edmund Ironside (average)

Q1 1016
Q2 Eadric Streona
Q3 Ealdgyth
Q4 Sigeferth
Q5 Battle of Assandun
Q6 Edward the Exile and Edmund Ætheling
Q7 Glastonbury Abbey
Q8 William Shakespeare
Q9 Malcolm III of Scotland
Q10 26

Cnut the Great (easy)

Q1 North Sea Empire
Q2 Sweyn Forkbeard
Q3 2
Q4 Denmark and Norway
Q5 Æthelred the Unready
Q6 1016
Q7 Lyfing
Q8 1026
Q9 Conrad II, Holy Roman Emperor
Q10 Poet

Cnut the Great (average)

Q1 Henry of Huntingdon
Q2 Harald II
Q3 Ælfgifu of Northampton
Q4 Edmund Ironside
Q5 Eadric Streona
Q6 Regent of Denmark
Q7 Trondheim
Q8 Norway
Q9 Rome
Q10 Magnus the Good

Cnut the Great (expert)

Q1 1016-35
Q2 Essex
Q3 River Thames
Q4 1018
Q5 Olaf II
Q6 Shaftesbury, Dorset
Q7 House of Knýtlinga
Q8 4
Q9 Wessex
Q10 Winchester Cathedral

Harold I (average)

Q1 Harefoot
Q2 Harthacnut
Q3 Æthelnoth
Q4 Earl of Mercia
Q5 Godwin
Q6 1040
Q7 Edward the Confessor
Q8 Alfred Aetheling
Q9 Westminster Abbey
Q10 Ælfwine Haroldsson

Harthacnut (average)

Q1 Half-brother
Q2 Denmark
Q3 1040-42
Q4 Emma of Normandy
Q5 Harold I
Q6 Coventry
Q7 Half-brother
Q8 Scandinavia
Q9 A wedding
Q10 0

Edward the Confessor (easy)

Q1 1066
Q2 House of Wessex
Q3 Westminster Abbey
Q4 Æthelred the Unready
Q5 Alexander III
Q6 Normandy
Q7 Winchester
Q8 Wessex
Q9 Archbishop of Canterbury
Q10 Coronation Chair

Edward the Confessor (average)

Q1 Edith of Wessex
Q2 Islip, Oxfordshire
Q3 Alfred Aetheling
Q4 Robert of Jumièges
Q5 Earl of Northumbria
Q6 Macbeth
Q7 Morcar
Q8 Emma of Normandy
Q9 0
Q10 Bayeux Tapestry

Edward the Confessor (expert)

Q1 *Vita Ædwardi Regis* (Life of King Edward)
Q2 13th October
Q3 1042-66
Q4 Rhys ap Rhydderch
Q5 Harald Hardrada
Q6 Edmund the Martyr and Richard II
Q7 Iceland
Q8 1017
Q9 Harold Godwinson
Q10 Magnus the Good of Norway

Harold Godwinson (average)

Q1 Battle of Hastings
Q2 1066
Q3 Battle of Stamford Bridge
Q4 Norman Conquest
Q5 Ealdgyth
Q6 Eye
Q7 Wessex
Q8 *Carmen Widonis*
Q9 Leofwine Godwinson and Gyrth Godwinson
Q10 York

Edgar Ætheling (average)

Q1 The Witenagemot
Q2 Kingdom of Hungary
Q3 Edward the Exile
Q4 2
Q5 1066
Q6 Never crowned
Q7 Malcolm III of Scotland
Q8 Robert Curthose
Q9 Uncle
Q10 Battle of Tinchebray

William I (easy)

Q1 The Bastard
Q2 2
Q3 Battle of Hastings
Q4 Rouen
Q5 French
Q6 3 months
Q7 Built castles
Q8 Church of England
Q9 Westminster Abbey
Q10. Robert Curthose

William I (average)

Q1 December 25th (Christmas Day)
Q2 Matilda of Flanders
Q3 Robert Curthose
Q4 Guy of Burgundy
Q5 1086
Q6 Battle Abbey
Q7 2
Q8 Lanfranc
Q9 New Forest
Q10 Riding a horse

William I (expert)

Q1 First cousin once removed
Q2 Herluin de Conteville
Q3 Pevensey Bay
Q4 1069-70
Q5 Isle of Ely, East Anglia
Q6 Treaty of Abernethy
Q7 1035
Q8 19
Q9 Earl of Kent and Bishop of Bayeux
Q10 Nearly 70 m

William II (average)

Q1 New Forest
Q2 *Rufus* is Latin for 'the Red' and he had red hair
Q3 0
Q4 The spot where William II fell after being struck by an arrow
Q5 Odo of Bayeux
Q6 Anselm
Q7 Malcom III of Scotland
Q8 First Crusade
Q9 *Anglo-Saxon Chronicle*
Q10 Winchester Cathedral

Henry I (easy)

Q1 The *White Ship*
Q2 2
Q3 The Anarchy
Q4 3
Q5 Normandy
Q6 Edward the Confessor
Q7 *The Coronation Charter*
Q8 Normandy
Q9 1135
Q10 Imprisoned

Henry I (average)

Q1 Duchy of Normandy
Q2 His brother (Robert Curthose)
Q3 To produce a male heir
Q4 2
Q5 He was returning from the First Crusade
Q6 Matilda
Q7 Anselm
Q8 Henry V, Holy Roman Emperor
Q9 Louis VI of France
Q10 Lampreys

Henry I (expert)

Q1 Reading Abbey
Q2 Maurice, the Bishop of London
Q3 1101
Q4 1106
Q5 Exotic animals
Q6 1130
Q7 Thomas FitzStephen
Q8 Fulk V, Count of Anjou
Q9 Bishop of Winchester
Q10 Philip I and Louis VI

Stephen and Matilda (easy)

Q1 The Anarchy
Q2 Uncle
Q3 Plantagenet
Q4 King Stephen
Q5 0
Q6 Second Crusade
Q7 Edith
Q8 Rouen Cathedral
Q9 1125
Q10 Peace

Stephen and Matilda (average)

Q1 Stephen of Blois
Q2 Eustace IV, Count of Boulogne
Q3 Matilda's son (Henry II)
Q4 William Adelin
Q5 Deeds of King Stephen (or Acts of Stephen)
Q6 Henry II
Q7 King Stephen
Q8 Flanders
Q9 Lady of the English
Q10 Gloucester

Stephen and Matilda (expert)

Q1 1135-53
Q2 His wife (Queen Matilda of Boulogne)
Q3 Oxford Castle
Q4 Faversham Abbey
Q5 Blois
Q6 St. Peter's Basilica
Q7 William de Corbeil
Q8 3
Q9 Battle of Ramla
Q10 William I, Count of Boulogne

Henry II (easy)

Q1 3
Q2 Thomas Becket
Q3 Plantagenet
Q4 Kingdom of France
Q5 Red
Q6 French and Latin
Q7 Winchester Cathedral
Q8 Ireland
Q9 Imprisoned
Q10 Jerusalem

Henry II (average)

Q1 Eleanor of Aquitaine
Q2 John
Q3 Treaty of Wallingford
Q4 Curtmantle
Q5 Louis VII of France
Q6 Angevin Empire
Q7 Perforated ulcer
Q8 High King of Ireland
Q9 Pope Alexander III
Q10 Count of Anjou

Henry II (expert)

Q1 Château de Chinon
Q2 1170-83
Q3 4
Q4 First (and only) English pope
Q5 1164
Q6 Edward Grim
Q7 William I (the Lion) of Scotland
Q8 Eleanor of Aquitaine (wife), Henry the Young King (son), Richard I (son), and Geoffrey II, Duke of Brittany (son)
Q9 English law
Q10 Fontevraud Abbey

Richard I (easy)

Q1 6 months
Q2 The Lionheart
Q3 Third
Q4 His mother
Q5 Acre
Q6 1189
Q7 Kingdom of Jerusalem
Q8 York

Q9 Saladin
Q10 The Pope

Richard I (average)

Q1 Aquitaine
Q2 Berengaria of Navarre
Q3 Philip II of France
Q4 Saladin
Q5 Chancellor of England
Q6 Their father (Henry II of England)
Q7 Jews
Q8 Sicily
Q9 Rouen
Q10 Crossbow

Richard I (expert)

Q1 Fontevraud Abbey
Q2 Burgruine Dürnstein
Q3 Hodierna of St Albans
Q4 Third Crusade
Q5 Anti-Semitic riots
Q6 The capture of Jerusalem by Saladin
Q7 High Sheriff of Nottinghamshire, Derbyshire and the Royal Forests
Q8 Arthur I, Duke of Brittany
Q9 Cyprus
Q10 Limassol

John (easy)

Q1 Great Charter
Q2 Lackland
Q3 Henry II
Q4 Innocent III
Q5 2
Q6 Dysentery
Q7 William the Lion
Q8 Runneymede

Q9 Stephen Langton
Q10 The First Barons' War

John (average)

Q1 Worcester
Q2 Angevin Empire
Q3 Ireland
Q4 Philip II of France
Q5 Robin Hood
Q6 His father (Henry II)
Q7 Arthur I, Duke of Brittany
Q8 Archbishop of Canterbury
Q9 Louis VIII of France
Q10 The Crown Jewels

John (expert)

Q1 Anglo-French War (1213–1214)
Q2 Isabella, Countess of Gloucester
Q3 Buy his loyalty while Richard I was away on crusade
Q4 He was the son of Henry II's eldest son, Geoffrey II, Duke of Brittany
Q5 5
Q6 1202-04
Q7 Marcher Lord
Q8 Henry II, Henry the Young King, Richard I, John, and Henry III
Q9 Llywelyn the Great
Q10 Welsh uprising of 1211

Henry III (average)

Q1 Henry of Winchester
Q2 First Barons' War
Q3 Kingdom of France
Q4 Eleanor of Provence
Q5 Earl of Leicester
Q6 Edward the Confessor
Q7 Jews
Q8 1259

Q9 Simon de Montfort
Q10 University of Northampton

Edward I (average)

Q1 Eleanor of Castile, Queen of England
Q2 Edward Longshanks and the Hammer of the Scots
Q3 Jews
Q4 Wales
Q5 Scotland and France
Q6 Ninth Crusade
Q7 Prince of Wales
Q8 Castles
Q9 First War of Scottish Independence
Q10 Smithfield

Edward II (average)

Q1 Hot poker inserted up the anus
Q2 Piers Gaveston
Q3 Robert the Bruce
Q4 Roger Mortimer
Q5 Hugh Despenser the Younger and Hugh Despenser the Elder
Q6 1322
Q7 Gloucester Cathedral
Q8 His son (Edward III)
Q9 Ordinances of 1311
Q10 Pontefract Castle

Edward III (average)

Q1 The Hundred Years' War
Q2 Nottingham Castle
Q3 Mistress
Q4 The Black Death
Q5 French
Q6 Edward of Woodstock (the Black Prince)
Q7 Philippa of Hainault
Q8 Battle of Crécy (1346) and Battle of Poitiers (1356)

Q9 Naval
Q10 John II of France

Richard II (easy)

Q1 White Hart
Q2 Westminster Abbey
Q3 Under a year
Q4 Edward III
Q5 14
Q6 Pontefract Castle
Q7 The Western Schism
Q8 Scotland
Q9 Wife
Q10 The Tyranny

Richard II (average)

Q1 2
Q2 Edward of Woodstock (The Black Prince)
Q3 Wat Tyler
Q4 Westminster Hall
Q5 Geoffrey Chaucer
Q6 Poll tax
Q7 Simon Sudbury
Q8 Hundred Years' War
Q9 Calais
Q10 Thomas of Woodstock, Duke of Gloucester; Richard FitzAlan, Earl of Arundel and of Surrey; and Thomas de Beauchamp, Earl of Warwick

Richard II (expert)

Q1 Kent
Q2 Savoy Palace
Q3 Chronicling the reign of Richard II
Q4 1386
Q5 William Walworth
Q6 1388
Q7 Bordeaux, Duchy of Aquitaine

Q8 10
Q9 1394
Q10 Charles VI of France

Henry IV (average)

Q1 Henry Bolingbroke
Q2 Nephew
Q3 Richard II
Q4 House of Lancaster
Q5 John of Gaunt
Q6 2
Q7 1399-1400
Q8 Lords Appellant
Q9 Henry Percy
Q10 Canterbury Cathedral

Henry V (average)

Q1 Henry of Monmouth
Q2 1415
Q3 Henry V and his heirs would inherit the Kingdom of France after the death of Charles VI of France
Q4 Surgeon
Q5 Lollard
Q6 Holy Roman Empire
Q7 1415
Q8 Dysentery
Q9 1
Q10 Edmund Mortimer, Earl of March

Henry VI (easy)

Q1 Kingdom of France
Q2 1
Q3 Catholic
Q4 Burned at the stake
Q5 The Wars of the Roses
Q6 Lancaster

Q7 3
Q8 Madness
Q9 English Channel
Q10 St Paul's Cathedral

Henry VI (average)

Q1 Margaret of Anjou
Q2 Tower of London
Q3 2
Q4 Notre-Dame de Paris
Q5 Edward of Westminster, Prince of Wales
Q6 Second Battle of St Albans
Q7 Windsor Castle
Q8 Louis XI of France
Q9 9 months
Q10 Hundred Years' War

Henry VI (expert)

Q1 Eton College; King's College, Cambridge; and All Souls College, Oxford
Q2 The Maid of Orléans
Q3 John of Lancaster, Duke of Bedford
Q4 1435
Q5 Duke of Suffolk
Q6 1450
Q7 The restoration of Henry VI in 1470
Q8 Her parents
Q9 Battle of Northampton
Q10 Maternal grandfather

Edward IV (average)

Q1 Edmund, Earl of Rutland
Q2 Elizabeth Woodville
Q3 2
Q4 House of York
Q5 George, Duke of Clarence
Q6 Edward of Westminster, Prince of Wales

Q7 1470
Q8 Richard Neville, Earl of Warwick
Q9 Herefordshire
Q10 Rouen

Edward V (average)

Q1 Richard of Shrewsbury, Duke of York
Q2 1483
Q3 Lord Protector
Q4 Ludlow
Q5 *Titulus Regius*
Q6 Tower of London
Q7 Westminster Abbey
Q8 Anthony Woodville, 2nd Earl Rivers (his uncle)
Q9 John Argentine
Q10 Thomas More

Richard III (easy)

Q1 Henry VII
Q2 Gloucester
Q3 York
Q4 Leicester Cathedral
Q5 Nephews
Q6 Thomas More
Q7 Yorkshire
Q8 Catholic
Q9 1483
Q10 *Richard III*

Richard III (average)

Q1 1485
Q2 White boar
Q3 Edward of Middleham
Q4 Richard Neville, Earl of Warwick (The Kingmaker)
Q5 Henry Stafford, Duke of Buckingham
Q6 Edward V

Q7 Wars of the Roses
Q8 1
Q9 Thomas Bourchier
Q10 1484

Richard III (expert)

Q1 University of Leicester
Q2 Northampton
Q3 *Titulus Regius*
Q4 William Hastings
Q5 Robert Stillington, Bishop of Bath and Wells
Q6 Thomas Stanley
Q7 Francis Lovell, William Catesby and William Ratcliffe
Q8 Idiopathic scoliosis
Q9 Lord Protector of England
Q10 Henry Percy, Earl of Northumberland

Henry VII (average)

Q1 Margaret Beaufort
Q2 Richard III
Q3 Pembroke Castle
Q4 Tudor
Q5 Wales
Q6 Lambert Simnel
Q7 Belgium
Q8 Arthur, Prince of Wales
Q9 Elizabeth of York
Q10 Uncle

Henry VIII (easy)

Q1 6
Q2 Protestantism
Q3 Faith
Q4 3
Q5 Monasteries
Q6 Kingdom of France

Q7 16
Q8 Charles I of England
Q9 Kingdom of Scotland
Q10 Ship

Henry VIII (average)

Q1 Jane Seymour
Q2 Anne Boleyn and Catherine Howard
Q3 Supreme Head of the Church of England
Q4 Thomas More
Q5 King of Ireland
Q6 Ferdinand II of Aragon and Isabella I of Castile
Q7 Pope Clement VII
Q8 Palace of Whitehall
Q9 Beheading
Q10 1509

Henry VIII (expert)

Q1 Laws in Wales Acts 1535 and 1542
Q2 1546
Q3 Catherine of Aragon
Q4 Henry, Duke of Cornwall
Q5 Non-aggression pact
Q6 The *Defence of the Seven Sacraments*
Q7 Anne Boleyn
Q8 Isle of White
Q9 Refuse the Oath of Supremacy
Q10 Richard Foxe

Edward VI (average)

Q1 Jane Seymour
Q2 Protestantism
Q3 Barnaby Fitzpatrick
Q4 *The Prince and the Pauper*
Q5 First cousin once removed
Q6 Edward Seymour, Duke of Somerset

Q7 15
Q8 Kingdom of Scotland
Q9 Hampton Court Palace
Q10 16

Mary I (average)

Q1 Roman Catholicism
Q2 Philip II of Spain
Q3 Catherine of Aragon
Q4 Bloody Mary
Q5 Lady Jane Grey
Q6 0
Q7 John Dudley, Duke of Northumberland
Q8 Wyatt's Rebellion
Q9 Thomas Cranmer
Q10 1558

Elizabeth I (easy)

Q1 Tudor
Q2 Anne Boleyn
Q3 Protestantism
Q4 Anglo-Spanish War
Q5 130
Q6 0
Q7 Privateer
Q8 Kingdom of Scotland
Q9 Kingdom of Spain
Q10 Leicester

Elizabeth I (average)

Q1 Mirrors
Q2 The Virgin Queen, Gloriana or Good Queen Bess
Q3 William Cecil
Q4 Mary, Queen of Scots
Q5 1588
Q6 William Shakespeare

Q7 *Golden Hind*
Q8 Christopher Marlowe
Q9 Francis, Duke of Anjou
Q10 Richmond Palace

Elizabeth I (expert)

Q1 Act of Supremacy 1534
Q2 Alonso Pérez de Guzmán, Duke of Medina Sidonia
Q3 Playwright
Q4 Margaret Bryan
Q5 Kat
Q6 The Succession to the Crown Act
Q7 25
Q8 Owen Oglethorpe, Catholic Bishop of Carlisle
Q9 First cousins once removed
Q10 Abd el-Ouahed ben Messaoud

James I (easy)

Q1 Robert Catesby
Q2 Scotland
Q3 Stuart
Q4 1611
Q5 1603
Q6 1
Q7 Anne of Denmark
Q8 Murder
Q9 Edinburgh Castle
Q10 State

James I (average)

Q1 Mary, Queen of Scots
Q2 Jacobean era
Q3 Combine them
Q4 The Americas
Q5 5th November
Q6 Henry Frederick, Prince of Wales

Q7 George Villiers
Q8 1618
Q9 Hung, drawn and quartered
Q10 Thirty Years' War

James I (expert)

Q1 Henry VI of England
Q2 *Daemonologie*
Q3 James Stewart, Earl of Moray
Q4 Lady Arbella Stuart
Q5 Isle of Lewis
Q6 1614
Q7 Architect
Q8 1613
Q9 Puritans
Q10 Plantation of Ulster

Charles I (easy)

Q1 The English Civil War
Q2 Scotland
Q3 2
Q4 1649
Q5 Oliver Cromwell
Q6 Thomas Fairfax
Q7 Carisbrooke Castle
Q8 England, Scotland and Ireland
Q9 The English Parliament
Q10 Beheaded

Charles I (average)

Q1 Henrietta Maria of France
Q2 Parliament
Q3 Commonwealth of England
Q4 Palace of Whitehall
Q5 The New Model Army
Q6 The Personal Rule (or the Eleven Years' Tyranny)

Q7 High treason
Q8 North Yorkshire
Q9 Prince Rupert of the Rhine
Q10 Henry Stuart, Duke of Gloucester

Charles I (expert)

Q1 Commission of array
Q2 The divine right of kings
Q3 William Laud
Q4 The Greyhound
Q5 John Hampden, Arthur Haselrig, Denzil Holles, John Pym, and William Strode
Q6 3
Q7 Scottish Covenanters
Q8 Anthony van Dyck
Q9 Battle of Chalgrove Field
Q10 The Rump Parliament

Charles II (average)

Q1 Titus Oates
Q2 The Interregnum
Q3 1660
Q4 Oliver Cromwell
Q5 Mistress
Q6 18
Q7 Assassinate King Charles II of England and his brother (the future James II)
Q8 Monarch
Q9 0
Q10 Battle of Edgehill

James II (average)

Q1 The Glorious Revolution of 1688
Q2 Catholic
Q3 James Francis Edward Stuart
Q4 1
Q5 Jacobite
Q6 France

Q7 William III of England
Q8 Louis XIV of France
Q9 Declaration of Indulgence
Q10 Brother

William III and Mary II (average)

Q1 William of Orange
Q2 Dutch Republic
Q3 James II of England
Q4 Protestantism
Q5 William III
Q6 Kensington Palace
Q7 1689
Q8 The Immortal Seven
Q9 Bishop of London
Q10 Henry Purcell

Anne (easy)

Q1 Great Britain
Q2 Westminster Abbey
Q3 Church of England
Q4 Stuart
Q5 Prince William, Duke of Gloucester
Q6 1702
Q7 Whig
Q8 War of the Spanish Succession
Q9 Jacobites
Q10 1684

Anne (average)

Q1 St James's Palace
Q2 Tory
Q3 1706 and 1707
Q4 Sisters
Q5 Denmark
Q6 Palace of Whitehall

Q7 Lord High Admiral
Q8 1703
Q9 The royal touch
Q10 Second cousins

Anne (expert)

Q1 Duchess of Marlborough
Q2 James II of England
Q3 Eyes
Q4 11
Q5 17
Q6 Speaker of the House of Commons
Q7 Whig Junto
Q8 Lord President of the Council
Q9 Thomas Tenison
Q10 1683

George I (easy)

Q1 Elector of Hanover
Q2 Robert Walpole
Q3 1
Q4 Scotland
Q5 He was German
Q6 James I
Q7 6
Q8 Spain
Q9 Cousin
Q10 James Francis Edward Stuart

George I (average)

Q1 Whig
Q2 Hanover
Q3 Great Turkish War
Q4 Mistress
Q5 Rioting
Q6 Ahlden House

Q7 In Hanover he was an absolute ruler; in Britain he had to rule through Parliament

Q8 Act of Settlement

Q9 A stroke

Q10 Lutheranism

George I (expert)

Q1 Osnabrück

Q2 54

Q3 Philip Christoph von Königsmarck

Q4 Triple Alliance

Q5 Chapel of the Leineschloss

Q6 Earl of Mar

Q7 7

Q8 His son, the future George II

Q9 Ernest Augustus

Q10 Louis

George II (easy)

Q1 Grandson

Q2 Adultery

Q3 43

Q4 The War of Austrian Succession

Q5 Westminster Abbey

Q6 British Museum

Q7 *Pirates of the Caribbean*

Q8 1

Q9 George Augustus

Q10 Prince-elector

George II (average)

Q1 Outside Britain

Q2 1745

Q3 French

Q4 His father (George I)

Q5 Frederick, Prince of Wales

Q6 Betty Burke

Q7 1756
Q8 He'd lived longer than any of his British or English predecessors
Q9 University of Göttingen
Q10 The sides of his and his wife's coffins to be removed so their remains could mingle

George II (expert)

Q1 Battle of Dettingen
Q2 Kensington Palace
Q3 Sophia Naturalization Act
Q4 George Frideric Handel
Q5 A string of notable British victories over French-led opponents during the Seven Years' War (The term is taken from Latin, and is used to denote a 'year of miracles' or 'year of wonders').
Q6 1759
Q7 Aortic dissection
Q8 Trinity College, Dublin
Q9 Golden Square
Q10 359 Georgia

George III (easy)

Q1 1801
Q2 King of Hanover
Q3 English
Q4 North America
Q5 15
Q6 Earl of Chatham
Q7 Boston Tea Party
Q8 Anti-Catholic
Q9 2
Q10 James Hadfield

George III (average)

Q1 0
Q2 Napoleon Bonaparte
Q3 Mental illness

Q4 His son, Prince George (the future George IV)
Q5 His father's (Frederick, Prince of Wales)
Q6 Enlightenment
Q7 John Stuart, 3rd Earl of Bute
Q8 The North American colonies
Q9 Thirteen Colonies
Q10 John Adams

George III (expert)

Q1 Norfolk House
Q2 *Cato, a Tragedy*
Q3 Duchy of Mecklenburg-Strelitz
Q4 John Stuart, 3rd Earl of Bute
Q5 John Wilkes
Q6 Lord North
Q7 Perth Agreement
Q8 The King of Prussia
Q9 Francis Willis
Q10 William Grenville

George IV (average)

Q1 The Royal Pavilion
Q2 10
Q3 Caroline of Brunswick
Q4 Brothers
Q5 Dissolve his marriage
Q6 1
Q7 St George's Chapel
Q8 Thomas Secker
Q9 Ireland
Q10 Tory

William IV (average)

Q1 Buckingham Palace
Q2 The 'Sailor King'
Q3 10

Q4 The Slavery Abolition Act 1833
Q5 Niece
Q6 Midshipman
Q7 To enable him to pay off substantial debts
Q8 Belgium
Q9 His brother (Prince Adolphus, Duke of Cambridge)
Q10 The electoral system

Victoria (easy)

Q1 Hanover
Q2 Husband
Q3 10
Q4 Europe
Q5 8
Q6 Great Famine
Q7 Corn Laws
Q8 4
Q9 Scotland
Q10 Crimean War

Victoria (average)

Q1 Empress of India
Q2 Isle of White
Q3 Albert of Saxe-Coburg and Gotha
Q4 Fifth
Q5 William Lamb, 2nd Viscount Melbourne
Q6 Lady Flora Hastings
Q7 Louise Lehzen
Q8 Haemophilia
Q9 Benjamin Disraeli
Q10 East India Company

Victoria (expert)

Q1 18
Q2 9
Q3 Kensington System

Q4 Dash
Q5 Ernest Augustus
Q6 400,000
Q7 Edward Oxford
Q8 1838
Q9 Felice Orsini
Q10 Because of a curt reply from the queen in response to some poetry he'd mailed her

Edward VII (average)

Q1 The Home Fleet
Q2 Second Boer War
Q3 Edwardian
Q4 Kaiser Wilhelm II of Germany
Q5 Parliament Act 1911
Q6 Liberal
Q7 Denmark
Q8 Buckingham Palace (born and died)
Q9 House of Saxe-Coburg and Gotha
Q10 Diagnosed with appendicitis

George V (average)

Q1 Charlotte Bill
Q2 House of Commons
Q3 HMS *Britannia*
Q4 House of Windsor
Q5 Mary of Teck
Q6 Balfour Declaration
Q7 1924
Q8 Tsar Nicholas II of Russia
Q9 1932
Q10 Charles Sims

Edward VIII (average)

Q1 1936
Q2 Sixteenth

Q3 Wallis Simpson
Q4 France
Q5 Duke of Windsor
Q6 Adolf Hitler
Q7 Serve on the front line
Q8 Kidnap Edward VIII
Q9 Windsor
Q10 Marguerite Alibert

George VI (average)

Q1 Second World War
Q2 First Head of the Commonwealth and the last Emperor of India
Q3 Albert
Q4 The Queen Mother
Q5 Speech therapy
Q6 Louis Greig
Q7 Prince George, Duke of Kent
Q8 Edward Wood, 1st Earl of Halifax
Q9 United Nations
Q10 Colin Firth

Elizabeth II (average)

Q1 Auxiliary Territorial Service
Q2 16
Q3 Sapphire Jubilee
Q4 Diana, Princess of Wales
Q5 Winston Churchill
Q6 Prince Philip, Duke of Edinburgh
Q7 Princess Margaret, Countess of Snowdon
Q8 Geoffrey Fisher
Q9 Supreme Governor
Q10 Grenada

Also by B.R. Egginton

Non-fiction

Edward VI: England's Boy King

Edward VI's Chronicle (Edward VI)

Richard II: The Tyranny of the White Hart

The Princes in the Tower: An Enigma… 500 Years in the Making

Nicholas II: The Fall of the Romanovs

Henry Hotze: The Master of Confederate Diplomacy

Historiography for Beginners

Archaeology for Beginners

Twelve Olympians: The Greek Pantheon Made Easy

History Essay Writing Basics: For High School and Undergraduate Students

Shorthand SOS: Learn Teeline Shorthand FAST

Public Affairs for Journalists: Concise Edition

Ice Hockey Rulebook

Fiction

The Sixth Number

A Kingdom of Our Own

The Chronicles of Ascension

History Quest: The Plot

The Prince and the Pauper: Annotated Edition (Mark Twain)

Trivia

The Ultimate History Quiz

The Ultimate Mythology Quiz

The Ultimate US Presidents Quiz

The Ultimate British Prime Ministers Quiz

The Ultimate British Royal Navy Quiz

The Ultimate French Monarchs Quiz